FOR BOYS ONLY

THE BIGGEST, BADDEST BOOK EVER

MARC ARONSON AND HP NEWQUIST

ILLUSTRATED BY

HEADCASE DESIGN

FEIWEL AND FRIENDS
NEW YORK

To my two boys, hope you like it.

—MA

To all of my nephews in the Newquist, Johnson,

Barranco, and Bradley clans. You guys rock.

—HPN

A FEIWEL AND FRIENDS BOOK
An Imprint of Holtzbrinck Publishers

Design by Headcase Design

Library of Congress Cataloging-in-Publication Data
Aronson, Marc.
For boys only : the biggest, baddest book ever / Marc Aronson, HP Newquist.
p. cm.
ISBN-13: 978-0-312-37706-9
ISBN-10: 0-312-37706-1
1. Handbooks, vade-mecums, etc.—Juvenile literature. 2. Curiosities and wonders—Juvenile literature. 3. Boys—Miscellanea—Juvenile literature. 4. Boys—Recreation—Juvenile literature. I. Newquist, HP. II. Title.

AG106.A76 2007
031.02—dc22
2007032847

Feiwel and Friends logo designed by Filomena Tuosto

10 9 8 7 6 5 4

www.feiwelandfriends.com

ACKNOWLEDGMENTS

Research is fun, but it helps when you can call on smart, informed people to share ideas and get pointed in the right directions. The following experts generously offered their time and their knowledge: Kevin Baker, author of a forthcoming book on baseball in New York; Dr. Jerome Cormello, professor of military studies, U.S. Army War College; Steve Case, About.com's skateboarding guru; Dr. John Hale, University of Louisville, authority on Vikings and their ships; Dr. Ross Hassig, scholar of Aztec armies; Jeanne Heifetz, expert on color names and their histories; Everett Howe, code master; Lee G. Miller, who did new detective work on the Lost Colony of Roanoke; and Kabir Nigam, who gave us a teenager's view of skateboarding and its heroes.

Thanks to Ken Wright for being such a good agent and nudging all of us in the right directions.

—MA

An author works hard to create a book, but it takes many people to make that book a reality. I want to thank everyone at F&F for producing the incredibly cool book you're holding in your hands, especially Jean Feiwel, Liz Szabla, Dave Barrett, and Karen Fein. Thanks to Ken Wright, who made sure that all things became possible. My ongoing gratitude to people who provided support and inspiration along the way: my parents, brothers and sisters, and their families, Michael S. Johnson, Thomas Werge, John Kunkel, Tucker Greco, Rich Maloof, Pete Prown, Lou Dobbs, and Darren Molony. And of course, all "the boys" from the not-too-far-distant past: St. Bridget's, Brophy, Phoenix, Notre Dame, the Skidders, the bandmates, the writers, and the guitarists.

While this book may be for boys only, there will come a day when you'll find that girls are a nice addition to our exclusive club. Hard to believe, I know, but it's true. So thanks to Trini, Madeline, and Katherine, because they're the girls who make it fun for me to be a boy.

There are many Internet sites and public libraries that provided me with much-needed information in the middle of the day and the middle of the night. There is no end to the astounding things you can find if you set your mind to it—look hard enough, and you'll find the entire world is waiting for you.

—HPN

CONTENTS

INTRODUCTION

"That is so interesting."

"Wow!"

"I didn't know that."

How many times have you said these things, when you landed on a neat Web site, or glanced at a magazine? Harvey and I are writers who love discovering new things. We thought it would be fun to have a whole book of the most interesting stuff we could find. Not a record book with endless tables of facts. We wanted a book that would be as filled with adventure and the unexpected, as all of the snakes, and battles, and sports cars, and ridiculously poisonous dart frogs we talk about. This is a book to get lost in, and find your own way out—and don't be sure that when you've read a page once, you've seen all that's there. Look again, look back, look ahead! There are things here to do, to see, to think about; codes to break, puzzlers to solve, even mysteries we couldn't figure out, which we hope you can. And while you do all that, we're gathering even more amazing entries for next time. —MA

Cool stuff is all around you—adventure, sports, animals, magic, warriors, movies, video games, and even danger. A lot of it you learn about in school and at home. But sometimes you just want the really good parts and nothing else, you don't want to sit through the boring junk. Marc and I know that—it's the way we've felt ever since we were kids. So when we wrote this book, we made sure it would have only the best stuff. We skipped everything else. And on those occasions where we had different ideas on what was the very best, we put it all in to let you decide. So there's something exciting to do, mind-boggling to figure out, and cool to learn on every page. We've got bloodthirsty barbarians, sports heroes, vicious predators, ancient mysteries, and daredevils all over this book. And that's just the beginning. It's a big world out there, with a lot of amazing things for you to explore. Welcome to the coolest place to start. —HPN

HOW DO WE KNOW ALL THIS STUFF?

We did a lot of reading and researching for all of the different topics in this book. We rode roller coasters, hunted down and talked to math experts, read books and Web sites on sports history, swam with sharks, and visited some of the Seven Wonders of the World. There are a lot of ways to do research, and we're pretty sure we did just about all of them.

There are a few *Reader Challenges* in this book, where we invite you to find answers to our persistent questions. Let us know what you learn, and we'll try to include it in the next edition. If you're up to the challenge, here are a few tips, based on the rules we followed in writing this book.

1. Always use more than one source for your information. That way, you can be pretty sure that what you've found is accurate. If you use only one book or one Web site, you can't be sure that some of their information isn't made up, out of date, or just plain wrong. Going to a few different places helps confirm that you're on the right track.

2. An expert in one thing is not an expert in everything. Your best friend may know a ton about baseball, but that doesn't mean he knows anything about the planets. Use books or Web sites that feature experts in the subject you're researching.

3. Some facts are open to interpretation, so try to figure out where each expert is coming from. Then you can make your own decision about what's important. We found experts who have different opinions on many of the entries in this book. They might measure the strength of venom in different ways (amount in a drop or amount in a bite) or disagree on the hottest spot on Earth (is it the place that has high temperatures through the whole year, or the place that had the one-day record for heat?). We wrestled with some of these facts—it was a lot like wrestling an alligator—and did our best to give you the most accepted interpretations of each of them.

4. Think of research as a game, and you'll have as much fun as we did discovering the amazing facts in this book.

READER!

BEFORE YOU START THIS BOOK,

STOP RIGHT HERE!

Are YOU ready for a Test of Skill and Daring that will Impress Your Friends, Awe Your Enemies, and lead YOU to be eligible to win some pretty cool Prizes?

We knew you were, so here goes. In order to give you a real challenge, the kind of fiendishly difficult test that only you could master, WE DEVISED A SERIES OF CODES THAT ARE CAREFULLY PLANTED THROUGHOUT THIS BOOK. And we searched the country and found a real Code Master TO DO IT. Our Diabolical Brain spends his days devising secret codes so difficult that the world's most powerful computers couldn't break them in a thousand years—and he's written some special puzzles as a challenge for *you*. You'll see some PUZZLES right away. The Apprentice Puzzles A are not only pretty easy to crack, they hold Hints and Clues—find as many of those as you can, because after that the road gets steep and winding.

The Apprentice Puzzles give you the equipment you'll need on your next quest: Find the fifteen Guardian Puzzles G . Solve them and you will have the keys to the Three Master Puzzles M . Pass beyond those gates and you can enter the Sanctum Sanctorum, the Mystic Land of the Ultimate, Great, and Final PUZZLE SUPREME ★ —crack that, and the SECRET WILL BE REVEALED (and remember, you could win stuff).

But beware, things are not what they seem. Our Big, Bad Brain does not believe you can untangle his dark and devious schemes and has laid many traps. Be Alert! Keep Watch, Clues May Lurk Anywhere!

P.S. The puzzles are here for extra fun; if you don't feel like puzzling today, that's OK, we also have snakes, cars, magic tricks, battles, pizza, adventures, skateboards....

SUPERCA

BUGATTI VEYRON
252 miles per hour
Zero to 60 mph in 2.5 seconds

Made by Volkswagen—the same company that makes the "slug bug" Beetle—the Veyron costs $1.2 million. The Bugatti brand has been around since the late 1800s, and this particular one is the most powerful supercar ever made: 1,000 horsepower, equal to more than 200 lawn mower engines.

KOENIGSEGG CCX
242 miles per hour
Zero to 60 mph in 3.2 seconds

Made by Swedish carmaker Koenigsegg, the CCX costs $755,000. New owners are encouraged to visit the factory in order to take special driving lessons on how to handle this four-wheeled beast.

MCLAREN F1
240 miles per hour
Zero to 60 mph in 3.2 seconds

Created by America's most famous racing team, McLaren, the F1 is the only American car on this list. It is no longer made, but whenever one is put up for sale by its owner (for a million dollars or more), McLaren Automotive rebuilds it for the new owner. There are only 64 of them in the world.

FERRARI ENZO
217 miles per hour
Zero to 60 mph in 3.2 seconds

Ferrari is Italy's most famous carmaker, and Enzo is the name of the company founder. The car costs $620,000, and buyers fly to Italy to have the car's interior custom fit to their bodies.

PAGANI ZONDA
C12 F ROADSTER
214 miles per hour
Zero to 60 mph in 3.5 seconds

Pagani is another Italian carmaker, and its convertible costs $690,000. The designer, Horacio Pagani, designed his first supercar at age 12 out of modeling clay.

SUPERCARS ARE THE FASTEST, MOST EXPENSIVE cars that can be driven on American roads. (Racing cars can't be legally driven on streets because of speed, safety, and noise concerns.) Mainstream car companies like General Motors and Nissan make millions of cars a year; supercar manufacturers make only a few dozen or a few hundred, and each one costs more than most people's homes. They are usually hand-built and require an elite team of physicists to design them so they don't fly off the road or burn up from the heat of their engines and brakes. Some supercars can outrun regular sports cars by nearly 100 mph.

Getting picked up from school in one of these cars would probably make the other kids—as well as all your teachers—stop and stare. Maybe even drool. So start saving your pennies for the coolest cars to ever hit the road. This is the supercar list you might want to have when you get your driver's license.

MERCEDES-BENZ SLR MCLAREN
207 miles per hour
Zero to 60 mph in 3.6 seconds

This is a car you might actually see driving around, as Mercedes is a popular brand in America and the price is only $455,000. This car was designed with the help of the same McLaren team that created the F1, above.

LAMBORGHINI MURCIELAGO
205 miles per hour
Zero to 60 mph in 3.8 seconds

Italy's Lamborghini makes supercars that can only be described as "wicked." This one costs $280,000. *Murciela-*

go means "bat" in Spanish and the first time this car was ever used in a movie was *Batman Begins.*

FERRARI 575M MARANELLO
202 miles per hour
Zero to 60 mph in 4.1 seconds

This supercar sells for $285,000. A Ferrari was featured in the Disney movie *Cars* as the dream car that the owner of the tire store had waited his whole life for.

SPYKER C12 LA TURBIE
201 miles per hour
Zero to 60 mph in 3.9 seconds

Spyker is an old-time race

car company in Holland, and it sells this supercar for $355,000. The car has no keys for the door or ignition; everything is controlled by a computer card. Each La Turbie has been sold before it was even finished.

ASTON MARTIN VANQUISH S V12
201 miles per hour
Zero to 60 mph in 4.7 seconds

This is the fastest car to come out of England. Aston Martins are perhaps best known as the cars used in James Bond movies, and this one sells for $260,000. The Vanquish was called the Vanish in the movie *Die Another Day* because it could turn invisible. Unfortunately, the real car can't do that—yet.

HISTORY'S WEIRDEST
DISASTERS

THE ELEPHANT STAMPEDE

People in Bhubaneswar, India, had always been respectful of the elephants wandering around their village. But in the summer of 1972, a severe drought left both man and elephants crazed from thirst. On July 10, elephants came rampaging out of the Chandka Forest and trampled the tiny village, killing 24 people.

THE BOSTON MOLASSES DISASTER

On January 15, 1919, a huge tank of molasses burst open at Boston's Purity Distilling Company. The tank was 50 feet high, and it spewed more than two million gallons of molasses out into the street.

A wave more than 10 feet high rushed down the street at more than 30 mph, swallowing up people and knocking buildings off their foundations. Twenty-one people were killed and more than 150 injured. To this day, residents of Boston say that you can smell molasses in the streets during the summer.

SNAKES FROM THE VOLCANO

Nearby residents watched daily as smoke and ash from Mount Pelee filled the air on the Caribbean island of Mar-

tinique. On May 3, 1902, the ash was so thick that people started evacuating, but they found their way blocked Hundreds of venomous fer de-lance snakes, along with biting ants and foot-long cen tipedes, had filled the streets—driven up from the ground by volcanic rumbling Fifty people and numerous horses were bitten and died before soldiers and feral cats killed the snakes. Two days later, the volcano erupted killing some 30,000 people Only two people in the town survived.

THE TEXAS CHAIN REACTION DISASTER

Texas City, Texas, was a bustling port town on April 16, 1947. That day, a ship ful

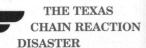

MONSTERS and DINOSAURS

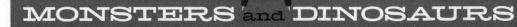

AMERICAN INDIANS WHO LIVE in what is now South Dakota tell tales of water monsters fight ing thunder spirits. The ancient Greeks believed that the griffin (body of a lion, claws of an eagle lived in Asia and guarded gold. But did these creatures ever really exist? In a way, yes. The Sout Dakota hills are filled with dinosaur-era bones, some from fins, others from wings. The Indian were just making sense of the bones around them. When scholar Adrienne Mayor went to the sup posed homeland of the griffin, where people went gold prospecting in ancient times, she found bone of Protoceratops—a dinosaur that had a beak, like an eagle or a griffin.

f fertilizer caught fire at the dock. Smoke from the fire attracted the attention of the townspeople, many of whom came to the water to watch. As the ship was being towed away, it exploded, killing more than 500 people. Windows in homes 40 miles away were blown out, and people felt the blast as far away as Louisiana. The explosion caused another ship in the port to erupt, and its explosion knocked a plane flying overhead out of the air. More than 5,000 people were injured in the disaster.

THE *EASTLAND* ROLLOVER

The *Eastland* was a 269-foot-long cruise ship docked in the Chicago River on July 24, 1915. The boat was scheduled to take 2,500 passengers on a picnic ride from downtown Chicago across Lake Michigan. As the ship was getting ready to depart, passengers rushed to its upper deck to wave to friends. The ship was already top-heavy (it had added extra lifeboats for the trip) and the weight caused the *Eastland* to wobble. It started to lean to one side, and then suddenly tipped over into the water. Although it was still attached to the dock and lying in only 20 feet of water, 844 people died in the accident, many of them sucked underwater by the huge wave caused by the falling ship.

HOW TO

FIGHT A SHARK

YOU'RE NOT LIKELY TO ever get attacked by a shark, especially if you don't go in the ocean. Living in the desert will keep you 100% safe.

The fact is that only about four people in the entire world are killed by sharks in any year. (More than 600 people die in the United States every year from falling out of bed or a chair. Sleeping and sitting may be more dangerous to your health than a hungry shark.)

Out of the nearly 400 types of sharks, only five are considered man-eaters: the great white, tiger, hammerhead, bull, and mako sharks. But let's say you come face-to-face with one of these teeth-filled beasts while you're minding your own business out there in the ocean. What do you do?

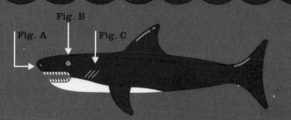

Fig. A   Fig. B   Fig. C

Punch him. Just like any bully, a shark hates to get punched. But you have to punch him in one of three places. Start with the nose *(Fig. A)*, out there in front of the teeth. Scientists think the tip of the shark contains extremely sensitive nerves that help it detect prey. So, punching it in the nose is like bashing its brain; it will get confused and wonder just what is happening.

If the shark is swimming by you, punch it in the eye *(Fig. B)* or up against its gill slits *(Fig. C)*. Again, these are sensitive parts of the shark, and sharks don't like having these parts touched, let alone punched. Dolphins have been known to fight off sharks by ramming their snouts into the gill slits.

Above all, DO NOT thrash around. Sharks are attracted to large fish and seals, animals that move around a lot, and the thrashing helps guide sharks to their dinner.

Also, try not to bleed too much. Those nerve endings are designed to detect blood in the water, and blood to a shark is a huge sign that reads...

"EAT ME."

ODDS

ODDS AREN'T PREDICTIONS, they're estimates of the chance that something might happen. But reporters use "odds" as if they were stating a future fact. Odds are figured out using mathematical formulas that consider how often things have happened in the past, as well as where and when.

Odds that you are reading this right now: 1 in 1

Odds that your house has at least one container of ice cream in the freezer: 9 in 10

Odds of being born a twin in North America: 1 in 90

Odds of writing a *New York Times* best-selling book: 1 in 220

Odds of catching a ball at a major-league ball game: 1 in 563

Odds of fatally slipping in the bath or shower: 1 in 2,232

Odds that Earth will experience a catastrophic collision with an asteroid in the next 100 years: 1 in 5,560

Odds of finding a four-leaf clover on the first try: 1 in 10,000

Odds of winning an Academy Award: 1 in 11,500

SPORTS

Q: *How can you hit a fair ball out of the park, and be called out?*
A: Jimmy Piersall was a good outfielder who did things his own odd way. In 1961, when he hit his 100th home run, he ran the bases in order—but turned backwards, his behind leading the way to each base.

As a result, Major League Baseball officials changed the rules. Now, you must run the bases facing forwards. If you copy Jimmy, you're out—and out of the game.

Q: *How can an umpire call a batter out and not out on the same play?*

A: Picture a batter up with runners on first and second and fewer than two outs. If the batter pops up the ball to the infield and the ump thinks a fielder would normally make the play, he can yell out, "Infield fly, batter is out!" The infield-fly rule prevents the fielder from deliberately let

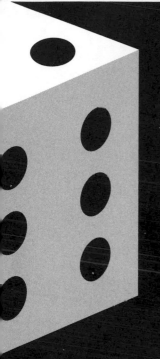

Odds of becoming a pro athlete: 1 in 22,000

Odds of being stung by a bee, or bitten by a snake or other venomous creature: 1 in 83,930

Odds of experiencing an earthquake: 1 in 100,000

Odds of dying in an airplane accident: 1 in 354,319

Odds of being struck by lightning: 1 in 576,000

Odds of dying from a dog bite: 1 in 700,000

Odds of being killed by lightning: 1 in 2,320,000

Odds of spotting a UFO: 1 in 3,000,000

Odds of becoming president: 1 in 10,000,000

Odds of winning a state lottery jackpot: 1 in 14,000,000

Odds of becoming a saint: 1 in 20,000,000

Odds of dying from a shark attack: 1 in 300,000,000

Odds of a meteor landing on your house: 1 in 182,138,880,000,000

ZZLERS

ing the ball drop so he can make an easy double or triple lay. But even if the ump calls he batter out, and the ball rifts foul and is not caught, it s just another foul ball, and he batter lives again.

: How can you score in foot- all if you get the ball when *there is no time left on the clock to run off a play?*
A: When a player calls for and makes a fair catch on a punt, his team has the option to try a field goal from the place where he received the ball. His team will have the chance to run the play, even if the clock reads 0:00. Not only

that, but they kick from where he received the ball, and the defense must start out ten yards away. The last team to score using this play was the Chicago Bears, in 1968.

MARK YOUR CALENDAR!

JULY IS NATIONAL ICE CREAM MONTH. Vanilla is the overwhelming favorite flavor, accounting for almost a full third of all the ice cream sold. (Chocolate is far behind, at 8.9 percent, and butter pecan at 5.3.) October is National Pizza Month—which makes it confusing that National Pizza With the Works Except Anchovies Day is November 12, followed the next day by National Indian Pudding Day—which shares time with Gingerbread House Day—all of which fall smack in the middle of National Split Pea Soup Week. None of which makes any sense, except that November 15 is National Clean Your Refrigerator Day—which, with all of that petrified ice cream, cold pizza, old pea soup, dry Indian pudding, and stale gingerbread lying around, is the only sensible choice.

WHAT DO YOU EAT?

CEREAL. AMERICANS EAT an average of 160 bowls of cereal per year. That means we slurp down about 1? pounds of cereal apiece. Which cereals? Cheerios are the big winner, followed by Frosted Flakes, and Honey Bunches of Oats. How come we eat those cereals? For one thing, advertising—one third of the cost of every box of Cheerios is spent on making sure you keep picking it, and so does your kid sister.

MOST POPULAR SNACKS FOR AMERICAN BOYS, AGES 8 TO 12

1. fruit
2. potato chips
3. chewing gum
4. ice cream
5. candy

BONE PRETZEL

LEAVE A LONG CHICKEN BONE to soak in vinegar for a week. The vinegar dissolves the calcium in the bone and makes it rubbery. When you take the bone out, you should be able to tie it in a knot!

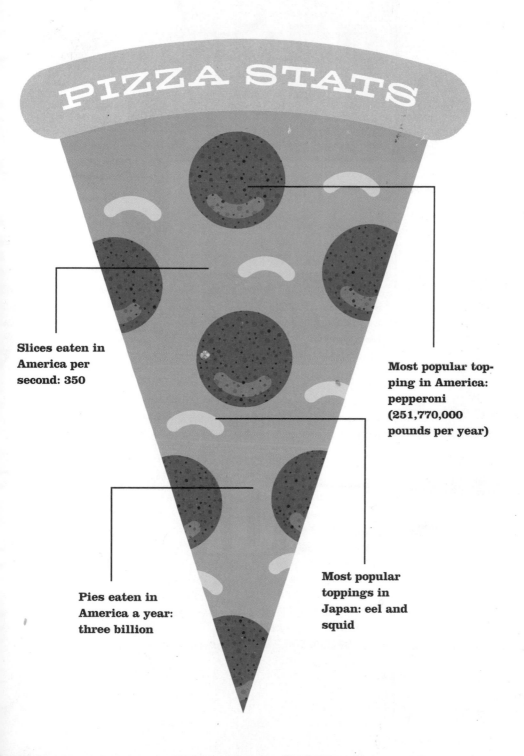

PIZZA STATS

Slices eaten in
America per
second: 350

Most popular top-
ping in America:
pepperoni
(251,770,000
pounds per year)

Pies eaten in
America a year:
three billion

Most popular
toppings in
Japan: eel and
squid

Bnlxwm qrwc oxa cqn Ducrvjcn ydiiun: Dbn cqn Ljnbja lryqna rmnj, kdc bqroc
njlq unccna xwn vxan cqjw cqn yanlnmrwp unccna.

DATES ?

1853

Potato chips invented at Moon's Lake House, near Saratoga Springs, New York. George Crumb, a cook, was annoyed at a guest who kept returning his potatoes complaining they were too thick. Crumb made them ultra thin, and invented the potato chip.

HPN: *Wait a second; back up here. Are you telling us that there were no snacks in America before 1853? That guys like George Washington only ate breakfast, lunch, and dinner?*

MA: *No doubt Washington's soldiers were dreaming of all sorts of goodies when they were eating "biscuit," a cracker that was either so hard it could break teeth, or moldy and infested with maggots. But until you had a country with a lot of people on the move, each region had its own separate snacks. If someone near you grew apples, you ate apples.*

1886

The drink that would become Coca-Cola first sold at Jacob's Pharmacy, Atlanta, Georgia, as a kind of medicine that would cure headaches, nervousness, and just about anything else that was bothering you.

1894

Dr. John Kellogg and his brother Will patent a formula for wheat flakes, then go on to file another patent for cornflakes. Breakfast cereals were first created as health foods.

HPN: *You know, cereal didn't always have sugar in it. I actually used to sprinkle sugar on Kellogg's cereal when I was a kid. When did cereal makers start coming up with the really sweet stuff?*

MA: *After World War II, lots of families had young kids, and there were plenty of ways to advertise on radio and TV. Sugar Smacks came out in 1953, each bite being more than 50% sugar.*

1904

Hamburgers, hot dogs, and ice-cream cones on sale together for the first time, at the St. Louis Louisiana Purchase Exposition.

75 86 16 47 02 46 F6 02 97 F6 57 02 76 56 47 02 77 86 56 E6 02 97 F6 57 0
D6 57 C6 47 96 07 C6 97 02 74 13 03 02 77 96 47 86 02 74 13 33 F3

O K N O W

M E R I C A

HPN: *I heard that the 1893 Chicago World's Fair introduced the hamburger, Cracker Jack, and Juicy Fruit gum. That makes Chicago a bigger monument to the joys of snack food, and even fast food, than a fair about the Louisiana Purchase, right?* MA: *The hamburger question is a fight. Check out this site: http://whatscookingamerica.net/History/HamburgerHistory.htm. They argue over what a hamburger is.* *OK, reader—settle it for us! Who invented the hamburger on a bun?*	**1904**
First pizza store opens at 53 1/2 Spring Street in New York City, though pizzas were already on sale in Chicago, where a man, whose name has been lost to history, was known to be walking through Italian neighborhoods carrying trays of pizzas on his head and selling slices to passersby. HPN: *That place in New York, Lombardi's, is still there. And they have tables and waiters, so you don't have to buy the pizza off of some guy's head.*	**1905**
Pop-Tarts are invented.	**1964**
First juice box in America. Ruben Rausing of Sweden invented boxes as a way to store milk. The rectangular containers were easier to stack than round ones. Rausing then figured out how to fill the same boxes with purified juices.	**1980**
Kraft Foods invents Lunchable packs.	**1988**
Pop-Tarts suffer a setback when it is discovered that they can burst into flames while being heated.	**1993**
Traditionally eaten with a spoon, yogurt becomes available in squeezable, single-serving tubes that kids can eat with one hand.	**1999**

HOW TO
LAND A PLANE IN

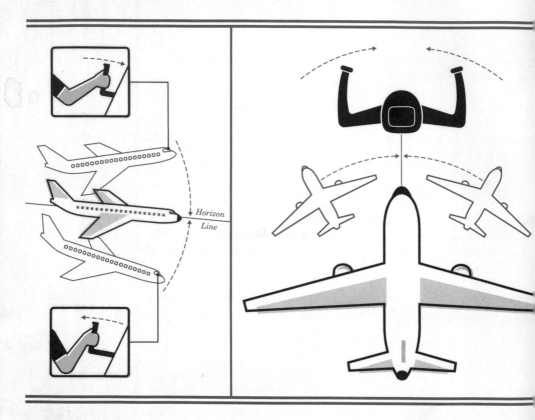

Horizon
Line

WHEN YOU SEE AN AIR-plane emergency in the movies, there's always some-one on the plane who can land it when the pilot gets injured. If this ever happens when you're on a flight, we think you should be that one passenger who saves the day. Here's how to land a Boeing 767, which seats about 300 passengers—all of whom are now depending on you to land.

Take the pilot's seat on the left side of the cockpit. In front of you is a steering wheel (known as a yoke). It turns left and right and pushes in and out. This con-trols your direction and whether you go up or down. The throttle, a lever or bar on your right, controls your speed.

Make sure you're even with the horizon ahead by looking out the front window.

If the horizon is below the window, push the steering wheel in to nose the airplane down. If the horizon is above the window, pull back on the wheel to get level.

Turn the wheel to make sure the wings are flat and even with the horizon. Once you're flying level, the plane will fly just fine. Now, there's a button on the steering wheel called a push-to-talk button. Press it and say

AN EMERGENCY

Mayday, mayday, mayday." This should put you in contact with an air-traffic controller.

Steer in the direction the controller gives you. When you get near the runway, make sure the plane faces it straight-on.

Put the landing gear down. Very important. The round knob to do this is located right next to your knee. Ease the wing flaps down a couple of notches; the flap lever is right beside the throttle. Make sure the speed brake, on the left of the throttle, is pulled back. This will turn on only when you touch down, so don't worry about anything happening right now.

When you get down to 500 feet, put the wing flaps down. Start reducing the speed by pulling back on the throttle. Keep the horizon as level as possible in front of you.

At the moment your wheels hit the ground, pull back full on the throttle to reverse the plane's engine. The speed brake should kick in automatically.

Remember, keep it cool, keep it level, and do everything easily and very slowly. Do this right and you'll be home in no time.

FUN MATH TRICKS

IF YOU'RE IN A REAL JAM with your math homework, these tips might just save your life.

ONE

All numbers are divisible by 1. Any number multiplied by 1 is still the same number.

TWO

Only even numbers are divisible by 2. Any number multiplied by 2 will always be an even number.

THREE

To find out if any number, no matter how big, is divisible by 3, add up the digits in the number. The sum will usually be a small enough number that you can tell if 3 will go into it (even 9,999 breaks down to 36, and you know that 3 goes into that 12 times). If that sum is divisible by three, then the original number is divisible by 3. If not, no way.

Try 1,544. Add 1 + 5 + 4 + 4. That equals 14. You know that you can't divide 14 evenly by 3, so 1,544 isn't divisible by 3.

FOUR

If the last two digits of any number are a number that can be divided by 4, the whole number can be. For instance, 681,224 has 24 as its last two numbers. 24 is divisible by 4, and so is 681,224. Note that any num ber divisible by 4 is always an even number.

FIVE

Only numbers that end with a 0 or 5 are divisible by 5.

SIX

If a number is divisible by both 2 and 3, it is also divisible by 6.

SEVEN

Take the last digit, double it, and then subtract it from the rest of the number. Let's do 224. 4 x 2 = 8. Subtract 8 from 22 and you get 14. That's divisible by 7, and so is 224.

EIGHT

If the last three digits of any number are a number that can be divided by 8, the whole number can. For instance 47,256 is divisible by 8 because 256 is. The way to tell if those three digits are divisible by 8 is a little trickier. If the first of those three digits is even, the number is divisible by 8 if the last two digits can be divided by 8

he 2 is even, and 56 is divis-
ble by 8, so the whole num-
er is divisible by 8. If the
irst digit is odd, subtract 4
rom the last two digits. If the
ast two digits are then divis-
ble by 8, the whole number
s. Let's take 368. Subtract 4
rom the last two digits (68 -
 = 64). Since 64 is divisible
y 8, the whole number will
e divisible by 8. Note that
umbers divisible by 8 are
lways even numbers.

NINE

o find out if a number is
ivisible by 9, add up the dig-
ts in the number. The sum
vill be a small enough num-
er that you can tell if 9 will go
nto it. If it does, then the orig-
nal number is divisible by 9.

TEN

Every number ending in a
ero is divisible by 10. Any
umber multiplied by 10 is
hat same number with a
ero on the end. 413 x 10 =
130. 6755 x 10 is 67,550.

ELEVEN

Here's a quick way to multi-
ly two-digit numbers by 11.
ust take the number you
vant to multiply by 11—let's
ay 53—add the digits
ogether, and put the answer
n the middle of that number.
 + 3 = 8, so 11 x 53 is 583.

TWELVE

f a number is divisible by
oth 3 and 4, it is also divisi-
le by 12.

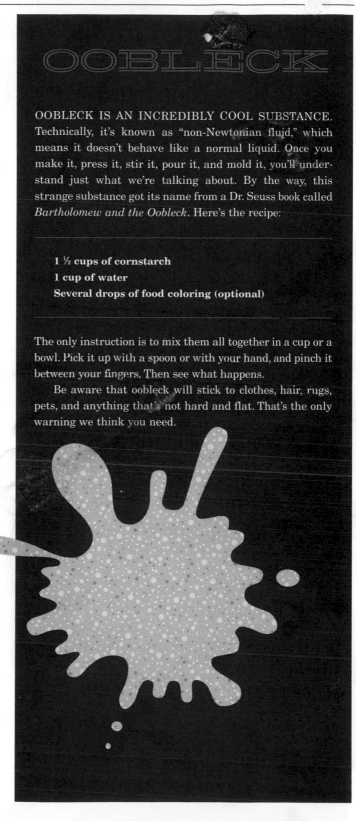

OOBLECK

OOBLECK IS AN INCREDIBLY COOL SUBSTANCE.
Technically, it's known as "non-Newtonian fluid," which
means it doesn't behave like a normal liquid. Once you
make it, press it, stir it, pour it, and mold it, you'll under-
stand just what we're talking about. By the way, this
strange substance got its name from a Dr. Seuss book called
Bartholomew and the Oobleck. Here's the recipe:

1 ½ cups of cornstarch
1 cup of water
Several drops of food coloring (optional)

The only instruction is to mix them all together in a cup or a
bowl. Pick it up with a spoon or with your hand, and pinch it
between your fingers. Then see what happens.

Be aware that oobleck will stick to clothes, hair, rugs,
pets, and anything that's not hard and flat. That's the only
warning we think you need.

MOST VENOMOUS SNAKES

THESE SNAKES HAVE THE MOST VENOM OF ALL SNAKES—one bite from a taipan has enough venom to kill a hundred people—but they are not always dangerous. The taipan lives far from humans, for example, and the sea snake is easily frightened away by humans. Some are large and lethal, almost 10 feet long, while others are not much longer than a common garter snake.

All venoms are poisons, but not all poisons are venoms. Venom is poison that is injected by animals into their prey, rather than a poison that is rubbed on or eaten by the victim. Snakes and spiders tend to be venomous, whereas plants and frogs are considered poisonous.

SNAKE	WHERE FOUND	AVERAGE LENGTH
Taipan	Australia	9 feet
Black Mamba	Africa	8 feet
Common Krait	Southeast Asia	5 feet
Australian Brown Snake	Australia	5 feet
Russell's Viper	South Asia	3 feet
Indian Cobra	South Asia	4 feet
Sea Snake	Australasian oceans	3 feet
Saw-Scaled Viper	Asia	2 feet
Coral Snake	North America	2 feet
Boomslang	Africa	4 feet

These snakes are listed in order of just how venomous they are.

MOST
DANGEROUS
SNAKES

ON THE OTHER HAND, THERE ARE PLENTY OF SNAKES that aren't afraid of people and are frequently involved in attacks. They may not have the most poison, but they're the ones that cause the most deaths and injuries. In the United States, about a dozen people a year die after being bitten by venomous snakes (although nearly 8,000 are bitten). Worldwide, some 50,000 deaths are reported every year, although some researchers believe that there may be 70,000 more deaths that aren't reported. Most of the deaths occur in Southeast Asia.

SNAKE	WHERE FOUND	AVERAGE LENGTH
Carpet Viper	India, Africa	2 feet
Russell's Viper	South Asia	3 feet
Asian Cobra	Asia	5 feet
Puff Adders	Africa	3 feet
Egyptian Cobra	Africa	6 feet
Black Mamba	Africa	8 feet
Common Krait	Southeast Asia	5 feet
Malaysian Pit Viper	Southeast Asia	3 feet
Tiger Snake	Australia	4 feet
Western Diamondback Rattlesnake	North America	5 feet

This is a list of snakes responsible for the most injuries and deaths, beginning with the Carpet Viper, which is involved in more attacks than any other snake.

EXPLORERS AN

DO YOU LIKE LONG WALKS? Check this out: In 1528, Estevanico—a slave from North Africa—landed in Florida with some 250 Spaniards. Their ships damaged by storms and under attack by local Indians, the captain quickly turned back towards Mexico, abandoning his men on land. So the men built rafts, and headed off into the Gulf of Mexico and reached what is now Galveston, Texas, some 750 miles away. From there, they began walking, hoping to reach a Spanish settlement somewhere. In eight years of walking through lands that were completely new to them, only four, including Estevanico, survived. They crossed all of modern Texas, turned south, and finally made it to Mexico City. They were safe, but the Spanish wanted to know more about the lands to their north. Three years later, Estevanico set off again, searching for the fabled Seven Cities of Cibola—but this time his luck failed, and he was killed.

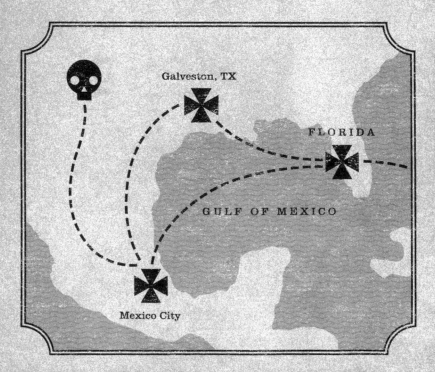

ADVENTURERS

"MEN WANTED FOR HAZARDOUS JOURNEY. Small wages. Bitter cold . . . Safe return doubtful." Twenty-seven men from throughout the British Empire and one from America responded to this ad, and joined Ernest Shackleton on a trip that was far worse than any could have imagined. In September of 1914, they sailed off from London in the *Endurance* to reach and then cross the Antarctic. But in January, they were trapped in ice, and would remain so for the next ten months as the ship cracked apart. The men spent another five months on the ice, then used lifeboats to sail to a barren island. Shackleton and five others then set out in a small lifeboat to cross 800 miles of raging sea to reach a whaling station and get help. When they reached land, they had to walk another 26 miles of frozen, rugged terrain. But they did, finally reaching the station. Then they returned to save the other men. Every single member of the crew survived.

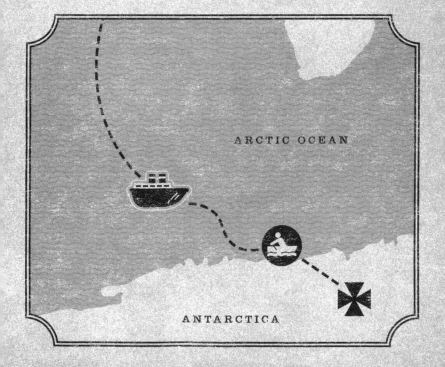

ARCTIC OCEAN

ANTARCTICA

NAURO ISL COMMANDER NATIVE KNOWS POS'IT HE CAN PILOT 11 ALIVE NEED SMALL BOAT KENNEDY

Carved on the side of a coconut, this message reached the U.S. Navy in August of 1942. Lieutenant John F. Kennedy and twelve men were riding in a small patrol boat named *PT-109* when their boat was sliced in half by a Japanese destroyer. Two men died, but the other eleven were left in the ocean on a moonless night, desperate to reach land. The men swam for hour after hour, and all the way, Kennedy carried along an injured crewman by holding the straps of his life preserver in his mouth. When one island proved to have no food, Kennedy led them out again to another whose coconuts kept them alive. A search party of Solomon Islanders found them six days later, and Kennedy sent a message back to the Navy with them by using that coconut. When he was elected president, Kennedy kept the carefully preserved coconut on his desk.

THE RACE WAS ON. The year was 1911 and Robert Falcon Scott, a British Navy man who graduated at the top of his class, was up against Roald Amundsen, a Norwegian who, ever since he was young, left his windows open at night to train himself to endure cold. This was not a contest with a starting line—each could begin where and when he wanted. For the goal was to become the first person ever to reach the South Pole. Amundsen chose a landing place for his boat on the Antarctic ice that was 60 miles closer to the pole than Scott's. Scott hit weather that was unusually brutal even for the polar region—temperatures that never rose above 0° Fahrenheit, and went down to -22°F. Even when blizzards blew through carrying warmer air, they only turned snow into impassable slush but, finally, on January 17, 1912, Scott and his four companions reached the pole. There, he found the flag of Norway: Amundsen and four others had gotten there 33 days earlier. Amundsen returned home safely, but Scott never got out of the Antarctic. He died in the snow sometime in March. Seven members of his party who turned back before the final trip to the pole survived, and his diary recording his final days was later recovered.

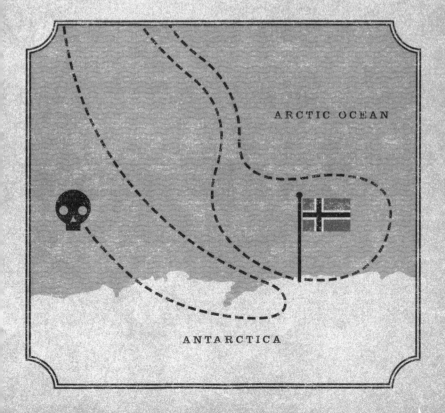

ARCTIC OCEAN

ANTARCTICA

ULTIMATE IN TEN SIMPLE RULES

1. The Field—A rectangular shape with end zones at each end. A regulation field is 70 yards by 40 yards, with end zones 25 yards deep.

2. Initiate Play—Each point begins with both teams lining up on the front of their respective end zone line. The defense throws ("pulls") the disc to the offense. A regulation game has seven players per team.

3. Scoring—Each time the offense completes a pass in the defense's end zone, the offense scores a point. Play is initiated after each score.

4. Movement of the Disc—The disc may be advanced in any direction by completing a pass to a teammate. Play may not run with the d The person with the d ("thrower") has ten seco to throw the disc. The defe er guarding the throw ("marker") counts out stall count.

5. Change of Possessio When a pass is not comple (e.g., out of bounds, dropp blocked, intercepted), defense immediately ta

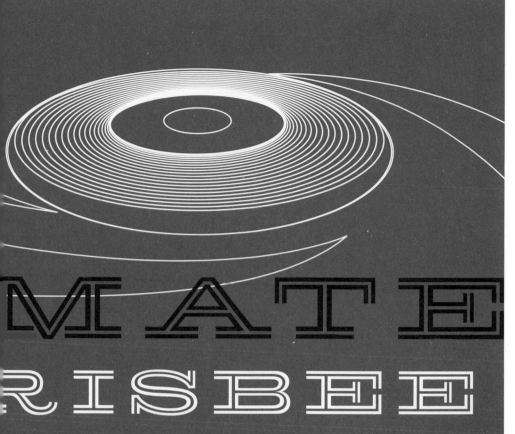

MATE
RISBEE

If you run out of games to play, just make up your own—like the kids who invented this one.

...ssession of the disc and ...comes the offense.

...Substitutions—Players not ...the game may replace ...ayers in the game after a ...re and during an injury ...e-out.

...Noncontact—No physical ...tact is allowed between ...ayers. Picks and screens ...e also prohibited. A foul ...urs when contact is made.

8. Fouls—When a player initiates contact on another player, a foul occurs. When a foul disrupts possession, the play resumes as if possession was retained. If the player committing the foul disagrees with the foul call, the play is redone.

9. Self-Refereeing—Players are responsible for their own foul and line calls. Players resolve their own disputes.

10. Spirit of the Game—Ultimate stresses sportsmanship and fair play. Competitive play is encouraged, but never at the expense of respect between players, adherence to the rules, and the basic joy of play.

Copyright ©
Ultimate Players
Association, 1993

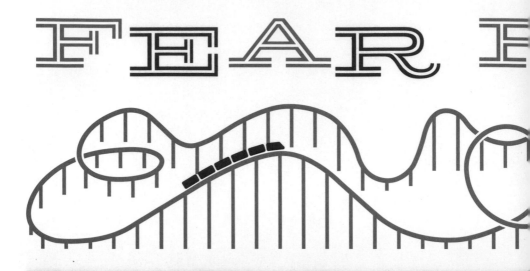

FEAR E

AMERICA'S SCARIEST

WHEN YOU GO TO AN amusement park, most of the rides are designed for fun, like the Ferris wheel and the bumper cars. But there are other rides that are designed to do something entirely different. That's to scare you so much that you'll scream like a newborn baby—maybe louder.

These are called "thrill" rides, because you'll be thrilled just to make it through them alive. Here are the scariest ones we've ever seen.

1. X-SCREAM
Top of the Stratosphere Hotel, Las Vegas, NV
The X-Scream is a huge teeter-totter on top of the largest freestanding observation tower in the U.S. You are lifted up and then over the edge of the tower, staring down 866 feet to the ground, before being yanked up into the air and going through it all over again. This is the kind of ride that will make even grown-ups wet their pants.

So is X-Scream this year's foremost outrageous ulti-mate ride? We think so. If you ride it, tell us whether you agree.

2. SKYCOASTER
Various Parks in the U.S. (including Lake Com-pounce, CT, Joyland Park KS, and many Six Flags parks)
On this ride, you are attache by a harness to a wire tha hangs between two tower The wire slowly pulls yo nearly 200 feet straight u where you are left hanging the air for several second Then you have to work up th courage to pull your ow release cord. When you d you drop straight down in free fall before the wi snatches you up and yo swing back into the sky like pendulum. You think you'

ACTOR:

USEMENT PARK RIDES

oing to die, then realize you
an actually fly.

, TOP THRILL DRAG-
TER AND KINGDA KA
edar Point, OH, and Six
lags Great Adventure,
ackson, NJ
nown as TTD and KK, these
re the fastest and highest
ller coasters in the world.
lmost identical in size and
nape, each one launches you
) stories straight into the
ky at 120 miles an hour.
nce your car hits the top, it
irves and starts spinning
efore free-falling straight
ick down to the ground.
his ride won't operate in the
iin because at such a high
eed raindrops feel like nee-
es flying in your face.

4. X
**Six Flags Magic Moun-
tain, Valencia, CA**
This roller coaster adds
something special to loops
and a 200-foot drop: You're
strapped into a seat backwards off the side of the
track. When you get to the
top of X and start speeding
up, suddenly, your seat flips
upside down and you're
screaming headfirst to the
ground. Since you're hanging
off the side of the track,
there's nothing between you
and the concrete below. And
just as your body is about to
scrape the ground, your seat
flips upside down again so
that you're facing the clouds.
The ride keeps flipping you
up and down, so you can't tell

if you're coming or going. Of
course, you'll be screaming
the whole time, so that might
not even matter.

5. INSANITY
**Top of the Stratosphere
Hotel, Las Vegas, NV**
Back on top of the tower next
to the X-Scream is Insanity.
You sit in a circle of seats at
the end of a long metal arm.
The arm then stretches out
64 feet over the edge of the
tower and spins so fast that
your seat flings out to face
the street and cars nearly a
thousand feet below. We
think it's called Insanity
because you might just have
to be insane to ride it.

DATES

ATTRACTIONS AND AMU

1786 The painter Charles Wilson Peale opens Peale's Museum in Philadelphia. In 1801, he mounts the first mastodon skeleton in America for display at his museum.

1841 Barnum's American Museum opens in New York—the place to see every thing from a fake mermaid to real Siamese twins. Two years later, Barnum expands his holdings by buying the exhibits of the bankrupt Peale Museum. Ringling Brothers Barnum and Bailey Circus is a direct descendant of the New York museum.

1846 Lake Compounce, in Bristol, Connecticut, opens as the country's first amusement park—the first attraction is an effort to blow up a raft with gun powder (which fails).

1859 Philadelphia charters the first zoo in America, though it does not open until 1874. This thing called the Civil War got in the way.

1873 The Mauch Chunk Switchback Railway—tracks in Pennsylvania originally used to haul coal down Mount Pigsah and Mount Jefferson to the Lehigh Canal—opens for business as a ride, the first roller coaster in America. Some thirty-five thousand customers a year flock to pay a dollar a ride to race down the mountain at 100 miles per hour.

1884 La Marcus Thompson opens the first amusement park railroad ride in the world, at New York's Coney Island. The short ride costs a nickel and takes passengers down a hill, then back up again. The ride does land-office business, and Thompson is hailed as the "Father of Gravity."

⊃ K N O W

N T   P A R K S   I N   A M E R I C A

eap the Dips, a wooden roller coaster, opens in Lakemont Park in Altoona, Pennsylvania. Though it closed for a time in the 1990s, it is back working again, and is the oldest roller coaster in the world that you can actually ride.	**1902**
oom period for roller coasters and thrill rides—Americans have money nd cars, so they are eager to rush off to find someplace to scream. And musement park builders provide even for those without cars—they build arks at the end of subway and trolley lines in big cities so everyone can et there.	**1920s**
othing is worse for amusement parks than the Great Depression (when merica's economy crashes and many people cannot find work), unless it s war. America enters World War II in December of 1941. Amusement arks do not really recover until the 1950s.	**1930s –40s**
isneyland opens in Anaheim, California.	**1955**
merica's first indoor waterpark with slides opens at the Polynesian Resort otel in Wisconsin Dells, Wisconsin.	**1994**

here and when did the first outdoor waterpark in America open? We've und candidates, but no proof—over to you, reader. Let us know what ou find out.

Thubird gubenuberubal hubint: Hubow dubo yubou cubount ubusubing hubexubadubecubimubal nubumbubers?

NATURE'S DEA

POISO

Fig. A	Fig. B	Fig. C	Fig. D
		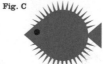	

POISON DART FROG (FIG. A)

Found in South American rain forests, this tiny, half-inch frog—smaller than a double-A battery—is the most poisonous creature on Earth. Just touching its skin will kill you.

CASTOR BEANS (FIG. B)

The castor bean (really a seed) contains ricin, an extremely potent poison. Eat-ing two of these seeds can be deadly, yet the oil made from them is regularly added to food and is also helpful in treating skin rashes and burns. Castor beans are grown all over the world.

PUFFER FISH (FIG. C)

These ocean fish contain tetrodoxin, a poison that affects the nervous system. Some people eat them as a delicacy (after the poison has all been—hopefully removed), but the poison one fish is enough to kill t dozen people.

BLACK WIDOW and th BRAZILIAN WANDERIN SPIDER (FIGS. D–E)

Two of the world's deadli creatures (spiders are insects), these two are in co petition for most venome spider. While there are m black widows than Brazili wandering spiders, the w

IEST

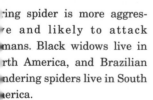
Fig. F

·ring spider is more aggres-
·e and likely to attack
·mans. Black widows live in
·rth America, and Brazilian
·ndering spiders live in South
·erica.

·ATH CAP MUSHROOM
·G. F)

·is mushroom is found in
·rope, the Americas, and Aus-
·lia. Eating a single mush-
·m can be fatal, and one of
· only cures is a liver trans-
·nt.

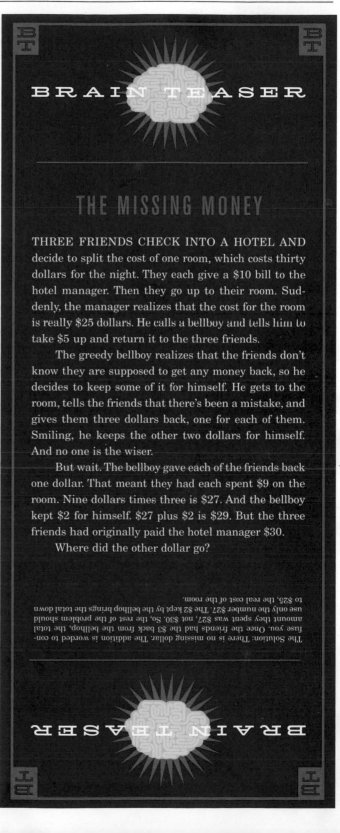

BRAIN TEASER

THE MISSING MONEY

THREE FRIENDS CHECK INTO A HOTEL AND decide to split the cost of one room, which costs thirty dollars for the night. They each give a $10 bill to the hotel manager. Then they go up to their room. Suddenly, the manager realizes that the cost for the room is really $25 dollars. He calls a bellboy and tells him to take $5 up and return it to the three friends.

The greedy bellboy realizes that the friends don't know they are supposed to get any money back, so he decides to keep some of it for himself. He gets to the room, tells the friends that there's been a mistake, and gives them three dollars back, one for each of them. Smiling, he keeps the other two dollars for himself. And no one is the wiser.

But wait. The bellboy gave each of the friends back one dollar. That meant they had each spent $9 on the room. Nine dollars times three is $27. And the bellboy kept $2 for himself. $27 plus $2 is $29. But the three friends had originally paid the hotel manager $30.

Where did the other dollar go?

The Solution: There is no missing dollar. The addition is worded to confuse you. Once the friends had the $3 back from the bellhop, the total amount they spent was $27, not $30. So, the rest of the problem should use only the number $27. The $2 kept by the bellhop brings the total down to $25, the real cost of the room.

BRAIN TEASER

THE STATUES ON EASTER ISLAND

RAPA NUI, ALSO KNOWN as Easter Island, is located in the Pacific Ocean, 1,290 miles off the coast of South America. Its inhabitants live farther away from other civilizations than anyone else in the world. Strewn throughout the island are at least 800 stone statues of giant heads with small bodies. Each one is carved from a single piece of rock, weighing as much as 80 tons and standing 30 feet tall. Scientists estimate they were crafted roughly 800 years ago, and are all from a single quarry on the island. But the current inhabitants of the island have no records of who actually built the huge statues or why. And no one knows how such huge stones could be moved from the quarry to distant points all over the island—some more than 10 miles away—without the help of machines or tools.

MA: *Ever read about Thor Heyerdahl? Really interesting guy, he had this theory about folks from Peru building boats out of reeds and sailing to Easter Island. He built Kon-Tiki, his own reed boat, and managed to cross the Pacific to the island. But scientists now are pretty sure he was wrong. Still, his books are fun to read.*

STONEHENGE

WEIGHING AS MUCH as 50 tons, the stone monuments at Stonehenge, England, are believed to have been everything from ancient altars and burial stones to an observatory for studying the universe. The huge stones are arranged almost like a circle of tables. No one is sure why these stones were dragged for more than 20 miles to this particular place, but archaeologists know that it happened for some reason nearly 5,000 years ago. And no one knows how the ancient people placed them on top of one another without the use of cranes or sophisticated lifting devices. Archaeologists believe that it took hundreds of years to complete Stonehenge, and that some of the stones may have been lifted by intricate wooden levers and hoists.

THE LOST COLONY OF ROANOKE

THE FIRST ENGLISH settlement in the Americas was established on Roanoke Island, Virginia, in 1585. Two years later, the first English child was born in what would become the United States. Her name was Virginia Dare. But in 1590, when a British boat came to bring supplies to the settlers, there was no one on Roanoke. Ninety men, 17 women, and 11 children had disappeared. Three chests left by the settlers had been broken open, with books, maps, and metal left exposed to the wind and rain. The supply crew found only one clue: the word "Croatoan" carved into a tree. As they knew, Croatoan was an area controlled by a nearby friendly group. Historians speculate that the settlers may have moved to Croatoan and blended in with the native peoples. But no one has ever determined for sure

GREAT MYSTERIES:
THEY LEFT BEHIND

what happened to the settlers or to Virginia Dare.

MA: *Dr. Lee Miller is an expert on this. She wrote a book about the Lost Colony. She told me she thinks the colony was sabotaged by one of its founder's rivals. And believe me, if you read about the guys from that time, they all had plots within plots within plots. So, it could be true.*

WHERE WERE THE ETRUSCANS FROM?

EVERYONE HAS HEARD of the mighty Roman Empire. But long before Rome became an empire, before it even controlled Italy, it had to defeat the powerful Etruscans. The strange thing is, no one is sure where this civilization, which introduced the arch, and perhaps even the system of law to the later Romans, came from. Were they sailors who arrived from Asia? Were they a local Italian group who simply developed their own culture? Scientists were sure the Etruscans were native to the Italian peninsula until DNA tests on Etruscan remains in 2004 showed them to have nothing in common with modern Italians and to be closer to peoples from what is now Turkey. We are back where we started — where did the Etruscans come from?

BADAKIZU EUSKARAZ?

BY STUDYING LANguages carefully, scholars have learned that some that sound very different actually have common origins. For example, English, Spanish, and Hindi are known to be part of a single, interconnected language group. But not every language fits into a group. High up in the Pyrenees Mountains between France and Spain live a people whose language is unlike any other. Though they borrowed words from neighbors, their language stands completely alone. The Basques keep to themselves, but before Columbus sailed, the Basques suddenly started to have a lot of dried fish to sell. Some historians think they found a route to North America, caught fish in the Atlantic, and dried them in what is now Canada. If they did, they certainly would never have told anyone. (Can you guess what the words above this paragraph mean? What would you ask someone to find out if he spoke your language?)

HPN: *The Pirahã tribe of the Amazon rain forest has a language that no one outside the tribe has ever been able to completely figure out. The people do not use syllables or tenses in their language and there is no written form of it. No one is even sure how they teach it to their own children.*

When you trace words back to their origins, it can get pretty interesting. An author named Jeanne Heifetz tells us that originally "blue"— the color of the sky— meant "to shine" or "yellow." So when we lived in caves, blue meant yellow.

WEAPONS
THAT CHANGED HISTORY

THROUGHOUT HISTORY, WHOEVER HAD BETTER technology could make better weapon
win more battles, and dominate their corner of the world. Here are some key technologica
advances that made big differences in battles, and even in civilizations.

BOW AND ARROW

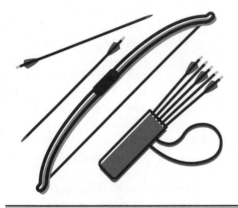

THE BOW THAT WON A BATTLE

October 25, 1415—Henry V of England was trapped in France with 900 sick, hungry, and tired soldiers and 5,000 bowmen to face a French force of some 20,000 men. Surprisingly, the Battle of Agincourt was a rout, won by the English. As French knights rode toward the English, archers using the longbow showered them with arrows. So many arrows rained down, it sounded like thunder. The 250-yard range of the bows allowed the archers to hit the French before they got close enough to fight.

HPN: *What makes a longbow any differen than a regular bow and arrow like the kin Native Americans used? And what were a those thousands of French soldiers arme with that allowed them to get beaten s badly—bad words and insults?*

MA: *The French had bows—in fact, their cros bows were very powerful, almost more lil guns than archery. But the French noblemen got all proud and defiant and charged ahead so while the English rained arrows down o the French knights, the French bowmen onl got into the action when it was too late.*

THE BOW THAT WON A CONTINEN'

The weapon responsible for the triumphs all the Mongol peoples (see p. 96) was the con posite bow. Each bow took over a year make, and was constructed out of wood, sine (such as the skin from animal necks), an horn. The bow was small enough to carry c horseback, and powerful enough to penetra leather armor. Until people figured out how make and use gunpowder, the composite bo was the most devastating military weapon the world.

STIRRUPS

STIR UP CONTROVERSY

And when stirrups first arrived, every fighter with a horse wanted a pair. That is because a warrior could wear heavy armor while brandishing his weaponry if he had somewhere to brace his feet. The poor slob with no stirrups had to wear lighter armor and use smaller weapons, or risk falling off his horse. The saddle with a stirrup made its way to Europe from China in the 300s. Some scholars think the humble stirrup created the entire world of knights in the Middle Ages. How come? Well, a knight in heavy armor on a horse was like a one-man tank; he could do all sorts of damage that no foot soldier could match. But to make the armor, feed the horse, and train the knight, you needed farmers to work the soil. Soon enough, you had knights, castles, and jousting—all because the stirrup could keep that man-encased-in-steel on horseback. But others say that no one invention could have launched the whole King Arthur package. We call this technological advance the footrest that transformed Europe—unless it didn't. What do you think? (Want more? Google "stirrup controversy.")

IPN: *Excuse me, didn't somebody in history start using guns somewhere? Seems to me that all those bow-and-arrow guys must have been pretty disappointed the day they first ran into bullets.*

MA: *For the longest time, guns were cumbersome, inaccurate, and hard to use. While the gunner was fiddling, the bowman was shooting. Guns were scary to guys who had never seen them, but not, at first, particularly dangerous.*

ENIGMA

THE ENIGMA THAT LOST A WAR

As Germany prepared to fight World War II, the Nazis were absolutely certain their secret messages would be secure. They sent messages using the Enigma machine, which took letters that were typed into it and translated them into other letters through a mechanism that produced so many possible variations, no code-breaker could make sense of them. But brilliant Polish mathematicians managed to figure out how the Enigma machine must have been set up, so they built their own copy of it. That was only a partial help, because the Germans kept changing and complicating their codes. Now the Allied fight against the Enigma went on two fronts: The British set out to capture Enigma machines from German ships or submarines, while, at the same time, teams of British and American code-breakers in a top secret project labored to decrypt Enigma messages. By the second half of 1941, the Allied team was able to break the unbreakable code. The information this yielded may well have decided the war.

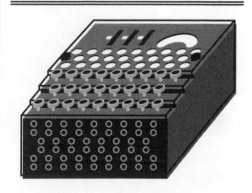

FAKE BLOOD

HERE'S A WAY TO MAKE REALISTIC BLOOD for stage shows, school plays, really gruesome Halloween costumes, or freaking out your friends:

- ¼ cup of creamy peanut butter
- 1 pint of white corn syrup (use the cheapest one you can find; they're usually thicker than the expensive ones)
- ¼ cup of dishwashing soap (try to use pink, yellow, or pale orange)
- 1 small bottle of red food coloring (these are usually .25 oz.)
- 5 drops of blue food coloring
- A clean quart jar or bottle

1. Add just ½ cup of the corn syrup to the peanut butter and stir until the mixture becomes runny.

2. To this peanut butter mixture, add dishwashing soap and the red food coloring. Mix everything together.

3. Add what's left of the corn syrup. Add drops of blue food coloring, one at a time, as you stir. The blue will make it look darker, so add as much as you want to make it look like your idea of the perfect color of blood.

4. Pour everything into the jar. Cap it and shake well. Now you'll have enough realistic blood to impress Dracula.

♠ ♣ ♦ ♥ CARD TRICK 1 ♠ ♣ ♦ ♥

"THE FLIPPED CARD"

ET A VOLUNTEER PICK A CARD, memorize it, and put it back in the deck. Casually search the entire deck and then, to everyone's surprise, find the volunteer's card.

. Take a complete deck of cards, and make sure all the cards are facedown.

. Flip the bottom card upside down so that it faces inward. When the deck is flipped over, this card looks like the top.

. Start with all the cards facing down (except the bottom one) and ask the person to pick one.

4. While your volunteer is looking at their card, casually flip the deck upside down. Now the only card facing down is your top card.

5. Have the volunteer reinsert the card in the same way they took it out. The volunteer will think that all the cards are facedown, just like theirs.

6. Flip the deck and spread them out, claiming that the volunteer's card has magically turned itself over. Make sure you don't spread them out so far that your top card shows. Their card will be the only one facing up.

HOW TO

ESCAPE FROM BEING TIED UP

YOU'VE DECIDED TO BECOME A SPY. But unfortunately, your latest mission has turned out badly. You've been captured, and now the bad guys are blindfolding and gagging you, and tying you to a chair. Here is what you need to do.

Quietly take a deep breath as you are being tied up. This expands your chest area, making your body bigger. Force your arms and legs away from the chair as the enemy is wrapping the ropes around you. If you can do it at the same time, flex your arms to make your muscles bigger.

When your captors have left the room, jerk your body so that you and the chair end up next to a wall. Rub your face hard against the wall (yes, it will hurt) so that the blindfold pushes up to your forehead and the gag drops down to your chin. Now you can at least see what you're doing, and you can yell for help if necessary. It'll also help your breathing.

Breathe out as much as you can and relax your arms and legs. The rope should now have a little bit of slippage because it's no longer tight on you. Wriggle your body, arms, and legs so that the rope gets looser and looser. Use your teeth if you can. It helps if you sweat, because that will make the rope more slippery. Focus primarily on freeing your hands because once they're free, you can get the rest of the ropes off that much quicker.

Now go save the world.

A SPY WALKS AMONG HIS enemy and sends back the information he gathers. A double agent convinces his enemy that he is a spy working for them. A triple agent convinces his enemy that he is a double agent working for them. Here are some agents who have done really well at this game of deception.

Karl Ludwig Schulmeister was a smuggler who was Napoleon's secret weapon. Schulmeister could change his appearance in an instant, and get out of any jam— trapped in one city, he escaped in a coffin. In 1805, Napoleon was at war with Austria. A native speaker of German, Schulmeister persuaded the Austrians that he was on their side. He fed them false information about Napoleon's supposed troubles, which he made convincing with fake newspapers the French printed up for him. Fooled by Schulmeister, the Austrians stumbled into a trap, and a 40,000-man army was captured. Collecting money from both the still-blind Austrians and the grateful French, he became a rich man.

The spy who had t[he] biggest effect on the outco[me] of a war may have be[en] Richard Sorge. Sorge work[ed] for the Russians during Wo[rld] War II. He posed as a Germ[an] newspaper reporter worki[ng] in Japan, which was alli[ed] with Germany at the tim[e]. When Hitler invaded Rus[sia] in 1941, Sorge's timely inf[or]mation told Russia th[at] Japan was not about [to] attack. Knowing that tro[ops] did not need to be kept in A[sia] to defend against Japan, R[us]sia was able to concentr[ate] on defeating the Germa[ns]. Though Sorge was fina[lly]

ught and killed by the Japanese, he is sometimes called history's greatest spy.

Then there is the spy family—where a sharp-eyed, seven-year-old boy played a key part, unfortunately enough, helping the Germans in World War II. In fact, the Kuehn family paved the way for the Japanese surprise attack on Pearl Harbor. Bernard and Friedel, their teenage daughter Susie Ruth, and then six-year-old son Hans Joachim arrived in Hawaii from Germany in 1935. Susie dated American sailors, even getting engaged to one. She and her mother ran a beauty parlor, where they collected information from the wives of military men. Hans would go on tours of ships and note details. Bernard sent all this information to the Japanese embassy by hanging different kinds of clothes on a line or flashing lights through his windows. The family was caught after the attack, but the damage was done.

The model for the suave superspy James Bond was a real double agent named Dusan Popov. He was recruited to work for the Germans during World War II, and gave them so much information they thought he was their best spy in England. But all along, he was actually working for England against Germany. Everything he told the Germans was almost true, but never actually valuable. He warned America about the attack on Pearl Harbor, but J. Edgar Hoover, head of the FBI, did not trust him. Popov was wealthy, enjoyed going to casinos, and dated attractive women. Ian Fleming, who later went on to write the Bond books, once actually met him.

SECRET MESSAGES

Could a secret message be contained in this sentence—without the use of any codes? Yes. Starting in World War II, spies developed the ability to shrink information into tiny microdots, the size of this period. Microdots could be hidden in any sentence, or on any postage stamp. You just needed to know where to look, and to have a reader that could blow up a tiny dot into a large image. Any microdots here? We aren't saying.

PUZZLE SUPREME

57 69 71 23 7B 66 79 27 6A 78 7C 79 2C 7C 7C 2F 84 79 73 87
34 79 77 8B 7D 39 83 89 3C 91 86 80 94 41 92 8F 85 88 8B 66

DETECT

IN THE OLD DAYS, DETECTIVES LIKE Sherlock Holmes walked around a lot, asked a lot of questions, and apparently always kept a magnifying glass nearby. That was about it.

Today, detectives have the entire world of science and technology behind them. Laboratories create products that make dried blood glow and can determine if two hairs came from the same person.

It's all part of forensics, which is the use of science to find solutions to legal problems. There are many ways that forensics are used in solving crimes, and popular TV shows like *CSI* have given people a close look at forensics in action. We've got a few forensic projects to get you started on your own investigations.

HOW TO

COLLECT FINGERPRINTS

1. Get some talcum powder or cornstarch (for surfaces like dark floors or desktops), or cocoa powder (for light surfaces like a window or the outside of a clear drinking glass); a small paintbrush with soft bristles; Scotch tape; a piece of paper (dark paper if you're lifting powder prints, white paper for the cocoa prints); and a magnifying glass.

2. Choose a hard surface and press your fingers against it.

3. Sprinkle talcum powder or cornstarch on dark surfaces and cocoa powder on light surfaces where there are visible prints.

4. Take a small paintbrush with soft bristles to gently swipe off the excess powder, leaving just the print exposed.

5. Take a piece of clear Scotch tape and press the sticky side down onto the powdered print. Gently pull the tape back and press it onto a piece of paper (dark paper if you're lifting powder prints, white paper for the cocoa prints). Now, you can examine the prints with a magnifying glass.

VE STUFF

CRIME SCENE INVESTIGATION

DENTAL EVIDENCE

LIKE FINGERPRINTS, PEOPLE'S BITE PATTERNS are different because every person's teeth grow in differently. (It can be a problem if criminals have fake teeth, though.) You can easily learn how to check for dental evidence. Have a few friends each bite a chunk out of their own individual apples, and then compare the bite marks. You should be able to see the differences in the position of each person's teeth. Then have them bite into the apple, but not take a chunk out of it. You'll see impressions of each tooth; compare them to check for differences.

CHROMATOGRAPHY

CHROMATOGRAPHY IS THE WAY THAT INVESTIGATORS identify ink, especially on fake documents. The process separates ink into different colors and determines which type of ink was used. Here's how you can do your own chromatography.

Fill a tall glass about one-third full. Take a pencil or stick and lay it across the top of the glass. Cut a piece of heavy paper towel into strips a little more than an inch wide. Take a number of different black and blue markers (some pen inks won't dissolve in water, so you need to use markers), and, using a different marker for each strip, make a large dot about half an inch from the bottom. Now drape the strips over the pencil or stick so that the dots are just above the waterline, and just the bottom touches the water—not the dot.

Let the water soak into the strips. As the ink dots begin to get wet, they'll separate into different colors, bleeding down the paper.

BLOOD
TESTING

THERE ARE EIGHT DIFFERENT TYPES OF HUMAN BLOOD. Blood is identified by whether it contains two components called A molecules or B molecules. Blood can contain one or the other, or both, or none. If the blood doesn't have either type of molecule, it's called O type. Human blood is known as the ABO blood group system.

By identifying the type of blood found at a crime scene, police can narrow down suspects by using percentages. That percentage is based on who has what kind of blood. Some types are more common than others. Here's how it breaks down:

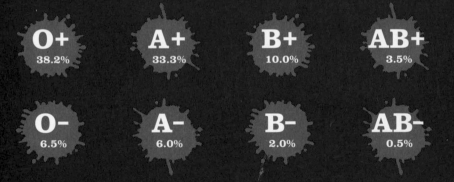

O+ 38.2%   **A+** 33.3%   **B+** 10.0%   **AB+** 3.5%

O- 6.5%   **A-** 6.0%   **B-** 2.0%   **AB-** 0.5%

The + (positive) and - (negative) refer to whether that person also has a particular protein in their blood. This is called the Rh factor, which is named after the rhesus monkey, who also has the same protein. People with the protein are positive in their blood group, people without it are negative. That's why some people have B-positive blood while others have type O-negative. Next time you visit the doctor, make sure to ask what blood type you have.

Let's say that type AB-negative blood is found at a crime scene. Since less than one percent of all people have that kind of blood, matching it to a particular criminal would make a strong case for that person being guilty. But if the blood was O-positive, which more than one-third of all people have, it means that the chances are pretty high it could have come from a lot of different people. That's where DNA testing comes in.

D N A
TESTING

DNA IS THE BASIC INSTRUCTION GUIDE FOR HOW YOUR BODY GROWS, and how you become you. All humans share similar DNA as part of our species, but one-tenth of one percent of your DNA is yours and yours alone (unless you're an identical twin). It is this small amount of DNA that is used to match criminals with crimes, missing kids with their parents, and determine the identity and the relatives of people who died long ago.

DNA can be taken from nearly any part of a person, including bone, hair, fingernails, teeth, blood, and saliva. When investigators arrive at a crime scene, they look for anything from which they can get DNA: a piece of gum, a half-eaten piece of pizza, the sweatband from a baseball cap, the inside of a mask. Blood is obviously one of the most common as it is often found on weapons or broken glass.

Then the DNA is tested in order to determine what makes up that tiny percentage that is unique to individual people. Once detectives have a list of these unique DNA components, they can compare them against suspects who have had their DNA tested. If a match is found, then it is pretty certain that this is the person they are looking for. The one problem with this is that if there are no suspects, investigators have no one and nothing to compare their DNA samples against.

HOW TO

GET OUT OF QUICKSAND

QUICKSAND IS THAT spooky stuff that seems to grab movie bad guys and suck them down to watery graves. It's not as bad as all that, but it is real. Quicksand is usually found near bodies of water, like lakes and marshes. It is a thick mixture of sand and water: Think of it like a sand milk shake. The thing to know about quicksand is that because it is part sand and water, it's very dense and most things will float in it. Including you.

If you find yourself accidentally falling into quicksand—maybe during a safari or secret mission—don't panic. Most of all, don't struggle, because flailing around will force your body downward. Simply remain calm, and let the quicksand push your body to the surface. Once you're basically lying on top of the sand, roll over and over until you reach solid ground. Or gently dog-paddle your way to the edge. That should take care of it, and will get you safely on your way. (You should also know that quicksand is rarely more than a few feet deep.)

WHAT ARE
YOU
REALLY WORTH?

YOU'RE WORTH A LOT AS A PERSON. Your friends and fam ily probably think you're priceless. But if you ever have to h any of your parts replaced, that actually costs real mor Here's what the hospital usually has to pay to get you so new parts, in case the old ones break down.

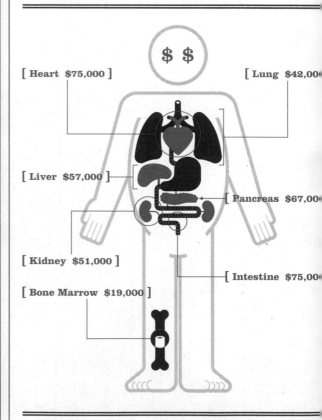

$ $

[Heart $75,000]

[Lung $42,000

[Liver $57,000]

[Pancreas $67,000

[Kidney $51,000]

[Intestine $75,000

[Bone Marrow $19,000]

Interestingly, there is no hospital price for the most import organ in your body, your brain. That's because brains can't transplanted. However, labs and universities pay about $ for brains to use in research.

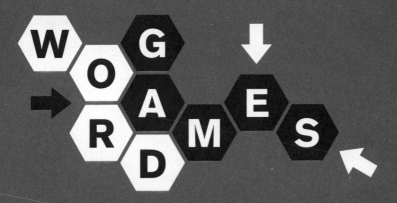

Palindromes are words or sentences that read the same way backward and forward. There are some everyday words you probably didn't know were palindromes: radar, Dad, Mom, ewe, eye, kayak, level, peep, rotator, stats, and wow.

Sentences are harder, but here are some great ones.

A man, a plan, a canal. Panama.
A Santa at NASA.
A Toyota's a Toyota!
Go hang a salami, I'm a lasagna hog.
Madam, I'm Adam.
Never odd or even.
No melon, no lemon.
Now I won!
Sit on a potato pan, Otis.
Was it a car or a cat I saw?

A **pangram** is a sentence that contains all the letters of the alphabet. The trick to making a great pangram is to keep the sentence as short as possible. You can even make up your own.

Bright vixens jump; dozy fowl quack.
Two driven jocks help fax my big quiz.
The five boxing wizards jump quickly.
The quick brown fox jumps over a lazy dog.
Heavy boxes perform quick waltzes and jigs.

C O D E S

THERE IS DANGER MAY COME VERY SOON

HOW DO YOU HIDE SOMEthing in plain sight? By using a code or a cipher.

You can make the simplest forms of code by lining up 26 letters in alphabetical order in one row, then starting a second row beneath it that begins somewhere else in the alphabet (*see* Fig. 1).

Suppose you want to send the message SEND HELP SOON. To encrypt this message, just take each letter and replace it with the one in the row beneath it. So SEND HELP SOON becomes FRAQ URYC FBBA.

This secret code is called a Caesar cipher, because Julius Caesar had his generals shift their messages back to him by three letters, so A became D. A cipher (like this and the substitution cipher below) is a code in which you scramble the individual letters of each word. There's one obvious problem with this: There are only 26 possible Caesar ciphers, depending on where in the alphabet you start the

second row of the table, so if your enemy knows you are using a Caesar cipher, he can try to decrypt your message using each of the 26 tables in turn. He'll be able to tell when he gets to the table that you used, because the decrypted message will make sense— decrypting using the wrong table will give gobbledygook.

You get many more possible ciphers if you don't write the letters of the alphabet in order when you make the second row of the table. You can just write all 26 letters in any mixed-up order you want . . . and there are 403,291,461,126,605,635,584 ,000,000 ways of doing this! When you scramble letters in this way, you are using a substitution cipher.

Somehow, of course, the friend you are sending your secret message to will have to know which scrambling of the alphabet you are using. You can either agree beforehand on a scrambling, or you can have a trusted messenger take the key to your code to

your friend. (Just make sure the messenger isn't a spy!)

But there are other forms of codes, too, where you replace entire words with other words. Commanders of submarines and ships used to have large codebooks that would tell them what words should be used to stand for others in coded radio messages. If the codebook said that SEND = HORSE, HELP = CHEESE, and SOON = MOSS, then SEND HELP SOON would turn into HORSE CHEESE MOSS. But again, everyone using the code would have to have the same codebooks with them. During wartime, capturing an enemy's codebook was one of the best things you could do—which is why naval codebooks were sometimes lined with lead, so that a sailor who was about to be captured could throw his codebook overboard and be sure it would sink to Davy Jones's locker.

In the story *The Valley of Fear*, the great (fictional) detective Sherlock Holmes was faced with a problem. An accomplice of the evil Dr. Moriarty, who wanted to

Fig. 1 A B C D E F G H I J K L M N O P Q R S T U V W X Y Z
N O P Q R S T U V W X Y Z A B C D E F G H I J K L M

betray him and warn Holmes of impending danger, mailed Holmes a coded message. But before he could send a second note explaining how to decode the first note, he was frightened by the sudden appearance of Dr. Moriarty himself. Holmes was left with the problem of decoding the secret message without knowing the key. The message began:

534 C2 13 127 36 31 4 17 21 41

Holmes tried out the idea that 534 might be a page number in a book—thus, a long book. If so, "C2" suggests "second column." Only a few kinds of books, almanacs, say, come in double columns and are common enough that Holmes would have them. Holmes and his companion Watson searched around, found the right almanac, and counted through the words on the page to find the ones given in the message: "There is danger may come very soon." And that is the fun part of codes—finding the secret message.

If you want to send a secret message to a friend and you haven't already agreed on a code or cipher, don't give up hope! You can always do what some ancient Greeks did: Find a trusted messenger. Shave the hair off his head. Write your message on his scalp. Wait for his hair to grow back. And then send him off to visit your friend. It's as easy as that! (But you should warn the messenger with the secret on his scalp to be very careful: Such extremely valorous emissaries need to evade enemy notice!)

♠ ♣ ♦ ♥ CARD TRICK 2 ♠ ♣ ♦ ♥

"THE MATH GENIUS MAGIC TRICK"

YOU LAY OUT ELEVEN CARDS AND ASK A volunteer to move several cards over from the right side to the left side while your back is to the cards (so you can't see how many are moved). When the moving is done, you turn around, wave your hand over the cards, and pick up one of them. It's the number of cards that the volunteer moved!

Take eleven cards from a regular deck. Take a joker, an ace, and one of all the numbers from 2 to 10.
Set up the trick by laying the cards facedown in this order: 6 5 4 3 2 Ace Joker 10 9 8 7.
Invite a volunteer to move any number of cards one at a time from right to left. The volunteer should be facing you on the other side of the table.

4. When the volunteer is done, count (to yourself) five cards from the right. With a wave of your hands, turn this card over. It will always be the number of cards moved. If it's the ace, it's one. If it's the joker, that means no cards have been moved at all.

The trick works because of the layout you set up, and because the cards are moved only from the right side to the left. This subtracts them according to the numbers on the cards.

(Try it yourself. Move four cards. Now the order is:
10 9 8 7 6 5 4 3 2 Ace Joker

Count over five cards from the right. Turn it over—it's the number 4!)

.... --- .-- -- .- -. .-.- ..-. . .- .-. --- -. .-. .. ... - ....- .--. .- -.. .- -.. ... .
.... .-.. .-.. -.-. .-. -- .- -- -.. ... .-

THERE ARE THREE ways to remember the presidents in order. You can work out a little rhyme where each word begins with the appropriate initial, but the ones we've seen are as hard to remember as the presidents and they don't include everyone. Like this:

Washington And Jefferson
    Made Many A Joke;
Van Buren Had Troubles
    Plenty To Find.
Pierce Boasted Loud;
    Johnson Gave Him
    Good Advice;
Cleveland Hail Cleveland
    Made Ruler Twice.

Write a memorable rhyme with the initials, in order, of at least 28 presidents in a row and we'll include it in the next edition.

Or you can try the location game—put the name of each president somewhere where you live—all around your

Remember that Grover Cleveland needs to be named twice since he was both the 22nd and 24th president.

house or apartment. Then try to picture that location in your mind. As you "walk" through the space you will "see" each president and remember the order.

But there is another way, which we've tried to help out with here—link each guy to something quirky, interesting, or memorable about him or his time. So instead of your room, you walk through our past. Crossing the bridge from Jackson to Lincoln—Van Buren, Harrison, Tyler, Polk, Taylor, Fillmore, Pierce, Buchanan—is tricky, because these are mainly guys who didn't accomplish great things. In fact, Henry Clay, who ran for president five times in this period and kept losing, is more interesting than all of them.

PRESIDENTS IN ORDER

1) George Washington (1789–1797) Started his military career in a botched mission for England in the Seven Years War, but later showed great leadership in battle and as president.

2) John Adams (1797–1801) Bright New Englander with a prickly personality, got on people's nerves, but opposed slavery. Father of No. 6.

3) Thomas Jefferson (1801–1809) Great writer whose words did much to define American ideals, but had no good answer for how to apply those ideals to the people he owned.

4) James Madison (1809–1817) Genius behind the Constitution, third Virginian president.

5) James Monroe (1817–1825) His "doctrine" warned Europe to leave the nations of the Americas alone

The two most tragic assassinations, Lincoln and Kennedy, both had vice presidents named Johnson. And that's not the only weird coincidence. Abraham Lincoln was first elected to Congress in 1846, John F. Kennedy in 1946. Lincoln was elected president in 1860, Kennedy exactly one hundred years later. Kennedy's secretary was named Evelyn Lincoln. Both presidents were shot on Fridays.

DENTS

ourth out of five first presidents to come from Virginia.

8) John Quincy Adams (1825–1829) Like his dad, his smart New Englander ad good ideas but no pizzazz.

9) Andrew Jackson (1829–1837) Bold personal-

president, and began the run of Ohio presidents, though also claimed by Virginia.

10) John Tyler (1841–1845) He called his Virginia home Sherwood Forest—making him Robin Hood—and he was such a go-it-his-own-way guy that his

being a sloppy dresser (useful if your parents keep bugging you about that) but died after being out in a lengthy July 4 celebration. Virginia's sixth, or seventh.

13) Millard Fillmore (1850–1853) When he split with his own party, he joined

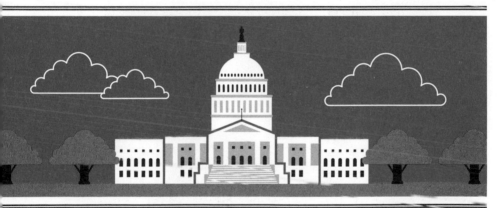

ty, easy to like, if you ignore ow he treated Indians.

) Martin van Buren (1837–1841) Known as Old Kinderhook after the New York town where he grew up, which some people think is the source of the phrase O.K.

) William Henry Harrison (1841–1841) Caught a cold while giving the longest nauguration speech ever, nd died a month later. He ad the shortest term of any

own political party rejected him. Virginia's fifth, or sixth—depending on how you count Harrison.

11) James K. Polk (1845–1849) President during the Mexican War, which added Texas and the Southwest to the United States, but made abolitionists mad, since the war was favored by slave owners.

12) Zachary Taylor (1849–1850) Known for

another called the Know-Nothings—whose anti-immigrant and anti-Catholic views were about as dim as the name.

14) Franklin Pierce (1853–1857) It took the Democratic Party 48 ballots at their convention to settle on him as their candidate—he was a last choice, not a best choice.

15) James Buchanan (1857–1861) The only president who never married, he was in office as the country slid toward the Civil War.

16) Abraham Lincoln (1861–1865)
He said the Civil War was fought to ensure the future of "government of the people, by the people, and for the people." To this day, that defines the best American political principles.

17) Andrew Johnson (1865–1869)
Took over after Lincoln was killed, and was extremely unpopular in the North because he seemed more worried about the rights of Southern whites than their

former slaves. (If you want to read more, try *Profiles in Courage* by John F. Kennedy.)

18) Ulysses S. Grant (1869–1877)
Great Civil War general but his presidency was marred by corruption scandals. Mark Twain later helped him publish his autobiography. Ohio II.

19) Rutherford B. Hayes (1877–1881)
Made a terrible deal when he agreed to give the South back to enemies of black rights so he would be elected. He may have been the first president to have his voice recorded, but no one can find the actual recording. Ohio III.

20) James A. Garfield (1881–1881)
Shot on July 2, 1881, by a man who was mad that he didn't get a federal job, he lived on until September 19. Ohio IV. (See a pattern?)

21) Chester A. Arthur (1881–1885)
First of the large presidents who looked like overstuffed seals, still, he proved to be a fair-minded guy.

22) Grover Cleveland (1885–1889)
Standing up to greedy, wealthy men and striking workers made him both popular and unpopular. No surprise that he won, lost, and won presidential elections. (*See also* No. 24.)

23) Benjamin Harrison (1889–1893)
Grandson of No. 9, he was the first president to have electric lights in the White House, which his wife was too afraid to turn on. He is also the first president whose voice has been preserved in a recording. Ohio V.

24) Grover Cleveland (1893–1897)
Thomas Edison filmed Cleveland as part of the inauguration ceremony for his successor—making him the first president in a movie. (*See also* No. 22.)

25) William McKinley (1897–1901)
The Spanish-American War took place in his first term. He was killed by a sick man in his second. Ohio VI.

26) Theodore Roosevelt (1901–1909)
Spanish-American War hero. A human dynamo, he ushered in the Pro-gressive Era by doing everything from creating national parks to shutting down monopolies. Like Jackson, a fascinating guy with terrible prejudices.

27) William H. Taft (1909–1913)
Biggest of the big presidents, he seemed dull and disappointing after T.R. He was much happier later in life as a Supreme Court judge. Ohio VII.

28) Woodrow Wilson (1913–1921)
People elected him to keep America out of World War I, but he ultimately led the country to fight in

t. He tried to speak on the adio, but was too far from he microphone to be heard— nd no one told him. With Vilson, Virginia either ties Ohio at 7, or takes a lead. For a very short time; guess where Harding was from?)

9) Warren G. Harding 1921–1923) An official he ppointed took bribes and vas caught. Harding was not orrupt, but the Teapot Dome candal defined his presiency. Harding was the irst president who people ctually heard speak on adio. Ohio VIII.

0) Calvin Coolidge 1923–1929) While the counry was in the lively Jazz Age f music, movies, and cars, it lected its dullest president ver.

1) Herbert C. Hoover 1929–1933) Despite being a mart, hardworking man, he ad no answer to the Great Depression that began just s he took office.

2) Franklin D. Roosevelt 1933–1945) Faced with ecoomic crisis and then World War II, he was the leader the ountry needed, declaring hat "the only thing we have o fear is fear itself." In 1939, e became the first president o appear on television.

3) Harry S. Truman 1945–1953) "The buck stops ere," said the sign on his desk, and it did; he made the decision to drop atomic bombs on Japan.

34) Dwight D. Eisenhower (1953–1961) In a time when people who had experienced the horrors of World War II wanted suburban homes, TVs, and new cars, he was a reassuring presence. A UNIVAC computer predicted he would be elected, the first time a machine accomplished that.

35) John F. Kennedy (1961–1963) Youngest president ever, which suited a time of rock 'n' roll, and young people joining the fight for civil rights. He and his opponent Richard Nixon were the first presidential candidates to debate on television.

36) Lyndon B. Johnson (1963–1969) Took over when Kennedy was killed and passed many reform bills, but could neither win nor end the war in Vietnam.

37) Richard M. Nixon (1969–1974) Famously "tricky," he was forced to resign when he tried to cover up his role in illegal acts against his political enemies.

38) Gerald Ford (1974–1977) Nice guy, great football player, calmed the country after the Nixon years.

39) Jimmy Carter (1977–1981) Better known today for his continuing work for world peace as an ex-president than for his term in office.

40) Ronald Reagan (1981–1989) Former movie star who mastered the use of the media.

41) George Bush (1989–1993) Father of namesake, who became 43rd President, and of Jeb Bush, who was the governor of Florida.

42) Bill Clinton (1993–2001) The first White House Web site was set up during his term—which is appropriate since he was known for his communication skills.

43) George W. Bush (2001–2008) The terrorist attack on September 11, 2001, defined his presidency. In 2004, bloggers first began reporting from presidential nominating conventions as they were taking place.

John F. Kennedy was the 35th president, his brother Robert F. Kennedy was a senator from New York who ran for president, and their brother Edward Kennedy is a senator from Massachusetts who also ran for president.

HOW DOES IT WORK?

SATEL

THERE ARE MORE THAN 3,000 satellites currently orbiting the Earth, although more than 5,000 have been launched since the Russians launched the first one, Sputnik, in 1957. Several thousand have already done their jobs and either crashed back to Earth or have broken up in space.

So how exactly do these thousands of satellites work? It's simple, really. They are designed to receive signals from the Earth (much like TVs and radios do) and then they transmit these signals to other parts of the Earth. Some satellites are as small as a basketball while others are more than 30 feet wide and weigh as much as a truck. Once built, they are loaded into rockets and launched to a specific point in space, typically around 22,500 miles over the equator, because at that point Earth's gravity is strong enough to keep it in place but not strong enough to yank it back to the gro Once released from rocket, many of them batteries or solar panels their power. Then th work begins.

Satellites receive in mation from a specific p and then send it back to ground. Ground station portable transmitters (those used by TV crews) the position of an indivi satellite and send electr signals directly up to it. satellite contains thousa

LITES

ectronic components that
ive the signals, add power
iem, and send them back
Earth. Receivers on the
ind get the signals and
n convert them back
heir original form (TV
vs, radio broadcasts, or
photographs of places in
r countries). You've prob-
· seen little round satel-
dishes on the outside of
ole's homes: These are
illite receivers for TV
vs and Internet connec-
s.

Of the satellites up above us (about 2,000 have already broken up or crashed back to Earth in the last 50 years), it's possible that as many as half are no longer functioning, making them nothing more than lifeless machines. Many of these will fall out of orbit and burn up in the atmosphere, while others just keep floating around.

NASA is tracking nearly 11,000 detectable pieces of space debris floating above Earth. These are satellites, as well as pieces of junk over four inches in size, including everything from nuts, bolts, and hand tools dropped by space-walking astronauts, to actual bags of garbage left by space missions, to pieces of exploded satellites and rockets.

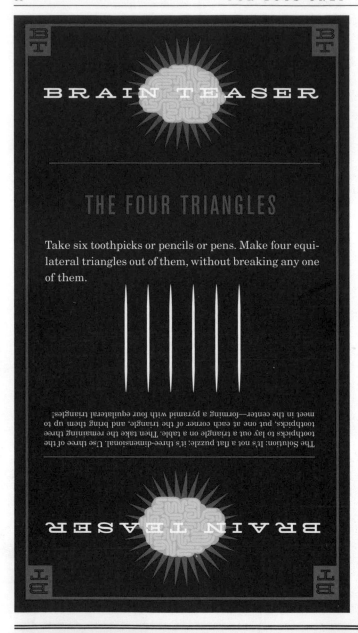

BRAIN TEASER

THE FOUR TRIANGLES

Take six toothpicks or pencils or pens. Make four equilateral triangles out of them, without breaking any one of them.

The Solution: It's not a flat puzzle; it's three-dimensional. Use three of the toothpicks to lay out a triangle on a table. Then take the remaining three toothpicks, put one at each corner of the triangle, and bring them up to meet in the center—forming a pyramid with four equilateral triangles!

LIQUID RAINBOWS

LIKE A MAGIC TRICK, this project suddenly produces swirling colors with no apparent reason. It's incredibly easy to do.

1. Take a pie plate or soup dish and pour ¾ cup of whole milk into it (2% is OK, but not skim or nonfat). Let it sit for about 15 minutes to get warm.
2. Put two drops of different colored food coloring in three separate areas of the milk (like two reds, two blues, and two yellows).
3. Add about four drops of dishwashing liquid into the center of the milk.

That's it. In a few moments, the milk will start churning and swirl the colors around. This happens because soap molecules attract the fat molecules in milk (which is why low or nonfat milk doesn't work well). As it pulls ever more molecules into itself, it causes the swirling in the plate, eventually pulling the food color in with it.

SECRET FOR DRAWING IN 3-D

YOU DON'T NEED TO TAKE ART CLASSES to learn how to draw things in 3-D. All you need is this trick:

Draw a shape (square, circle, triangle, almost anything) and then draw it again an inch or two away. Then connect the same points on each shape with a straight line. That's all it takes.

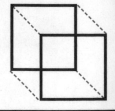

HOW TO

WIN AT ROCK, PAPER, SCISSORS

LOOK AT THE GUY YOU ARE PLAYING. Is he the kind of person who thinks rocks are strong and paper is weak? Try to guess what he is going to lead with. Confuse your enemy: He is looking at you, wondering if you like rocks. So, pick a strategy that you will follow no matter what. You could go:

Rock, Rock, Rock
Paper, Paper, Paper,
Rock, Paper, Scissors
Scissors, Rock, Paper

Not hard to figure out the rest. But if you program yourself ahead of time and read your enemy, you'll have the best chance to win.

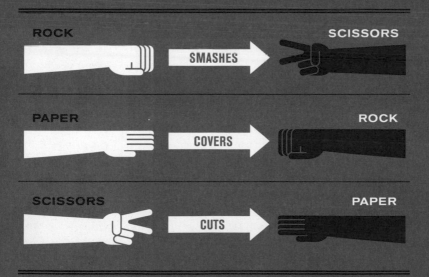

TOP ELEVEN
GREATEST MOMENT

BASEBALL

IT'S EVERY BASEBALL player's dream: In one swing, with the pressure on, you win the World Series. Two series have ended with home runs, one with a home run in the bottom of the ninth inning of the seventh game: In 1960, Bill Mazerowski—the great second baseman for the Pittsburgh Pirates—hit a 1-0 pitch from Yankee Ralph Terry over the wall to win the game and the series.

In 1993, Joe Carter of Toronto hit a three-run homer to beat Philadelphia and win the World Series. It was again the bottom of the ninth, but this was the sixth game. Carter took a 2-2 pitch over the fence, ending the series.

The fifth game of the 1956 World Series was the greatest game ever pitched. Don Larson of the Yankees took a perfect game into the ninth inning, retired the first two batters, and had a 1-2 count on the third. With the 97th pitch of the game, he caught Dale Mitchell looking, the 27th Dodger in a row. To this day, Dodger fans claim the pitch was high. So what?

It would have been 2-2.

But then again, no one can or will ever make a greater play than Willie Mays of the New York Giants did in game one of the 1954 World Series. The Giants played in the Polo Grounds, a stadium whose outfield went on forever—today, dead center is usually about 410 feet from home; in the Polo Grounds it was 475. Running at full speed, his back to the plate, Mays caught a line drive hit by Vic Wertz of the Cleveland Indians that had gone more than 400 feet. That was amazing, but the superhuman part was the throw—even as he caught the ball, he began turning, spinning back so that he could get enough power on his throw to hold Al Rosen on first base. The catch was dazzling, the throw superhuman. The Giants went on to sweep the series.

HOCKEY

THE 1980 U.S. OLYMPIC Hockey team had no chance against the Soviet Union. The Soviet team had beaten the best players in the NHL 6-0, and the American

Olympians themselves 10- in exhibition matches. Bu battling back after trailing 1 0, 2-1, and 3-2, the American finally took a 4-3 lead in th third period on Mike Eru zione's slap shot. Unbeliev ably, against any logic, th lead held, until announcer A Michaels counted down th last seconds, "Five seconds t go in the game. . . . Do yo believe in miracles? YES!" T this day, if you watch th tape, it really does seer miraculous.

HPN: *I'll admit, this is th sentimental favorite. Bu the real greatest moment i hockey—maybe in an sport—came during th Stanley Cup Finals betwee the Boston Bruins and the S Louis Blues on May 10, 197 The Bruins' Bobby Orr, num ber 4, scored the fourth go in the fourth period (over time) of the fourth game win the championship— while flying through the a after being tripped by No Picard. Oh, Picard's num ber? 4. Still gives me the chill*

MA: *That is the sad fate hockey fans—you love th wonderful sport with a gre*

N SPORTS HISTORY

istory, but no one else
nows about it.

BASKETBALL

THE SHOT THAT
Christian Laettner made
to give Duke the eastern
regional final victory in the
1992 NCAA tournament
simply was not possible.
Duke was down to Kentucky
103-102 with 2.1 seconds left
in overtime. They had the
ball under their own basket,
to first, Grant Hill had to
throw a perfect, 80-foot pass
over all of the waving Kentucky hands. Then Laettner
had to catch it, fake to get
free, and shoot a sweet 17-
footer as time expired—cap-
ping a day in which he shot
1-11 from the field, and 10-
10 from the line. Duke won,
Kentucky cried.

Good for Christian, but
how about Michael Jordan's
play in the last 41 seconds of
the sixth game of the 1998
NBA Finals? Chicago was up
three games to two over
Utah. Win this and they'd
have their sixth title in eight
years. But the Bulls were
down 86-83. First, Jordan hit
a shot—86-85. Then he cir-
cled back to strip the ball

from Utah's star, Karl "the
Mailman" Malone. With seconds ticking off, Jordan faced
one of the best defenders on
the Jazz, faked him (or, some
say, pushed him), got free,
and hit the winning basket.
Chicago reigned again.

HPN: *Hey, don't forget football. I see Doug Flutie's pass
on page 69, but how could
you leave out Stanford versus California on November
20, 1982? Stanford kicked a
field goal with eight seconds
left to play and took the lead
by one point, 20-19. They were
sure they'd won the game,
and so was everyone else.
With four seconds on the
clock, Cal took the final kick-
off, and returned the ball
downfield by lateraling five
times and running right
through the Stanford band,
which had taken the field
thinking their team had
already won. Cal scored a
touchdown with no time left,
and beat Stanford 25-20.
They don't call this one "The
Play" for nothing.*

MA: *The Play is like the 1972
Olympic Gold Medal basketball game (see page 67).
Stanford fans still don't*
*agree that it was legal, and
spend endless time going
over tape to prove that one of
those tosses was an illegal
forward lateral, or someone
had his knee down and was
touched. . . . I like having
instant replay and all, but
sometimes that just leads to
more arguments that go on
and on, and on into the next
century.*

SOCCER

ENGLAND AND ARGEN-
tina fought a strange
war in 1982 over a group of
islands. Four years later, they
met in a World Cup quarter-
final. Argentina's Diego
Maradona scored the first
goal—actually his hand did;
it was an illegal play. But the
second and deciding goal was
voted the greatest goal in
World Cup history. Maradona
held the ball for ten seconds,
weaving through five English
defenders before shooting it
past the goalie. Argentina
won 2-1. They'd lost the
Falkland Islands, but went
on to take the World Cup.

ATH
WHO CHANGE
LIT

TWO ATHLETES AND ONE TEAM CHANGED HISTORY WITH THEIR VICTORIES.

In 1936, Germany hosted the Summer Olympics—a great chance to display what they believed was the superiority of Germans. But they didn't reckon on American Jesse Owens. Born poor in Alabama, he made himself into the world's greatest run-

ner. Owens won the gold in four events, setting Olympic records in the 100 meters, the long jump, and the 200 meters. He also led off the U.S. gold-medal-winning 4 X 100 relay team. The Nazis were free to go home and sulk.

SONNY LISTON HAD lived a hard life—born the 24th of 25 kids, he grew up extremely poor. He made his way with his fists,

always on the edge of crim Liston was the boxer as bully, the man you woul never want to meet in a dar alley. On February 25, 196 he went into the ring a 7-favorite over the challenger, young boxer named Cassi Clay. Clay wove, dance taunted, and spun aroun Liston, until in the sevent round, when the heavy weight champion gave u Clay changed his name

LETES THE WORLD — ERALLY

Muhammad Ali, and to millions of people around the country and the world who watched and listened, his fight showed that times were changing—youth, brains, and confidence could beat any odds.

IT WAS REALLY EASY TO tell apart the two teams in the 1966 NCAA Final: Kentucky's players were all white, and they were the proud inheritors of a tradition of great white basketball teams at the school. The five starters for Texas Western were all black—the first all-black starting five in NCAA Finals history. Kentucky was favored—for all the reasons prejudice dictated—supposedly, they were more disciplined, whereas TW was going to be too flashy and fall apart under pressure.

Just the opposite happened: TW did a better job of passing, controlling the ball, and playing defense, and won 72-65. From then on, the days of segregation in basketball were numbered. A movie about that year and that game is called *Glory Road*.

COMEBACK-UPSE

DUE TO WORLD WAR II, the 1950 World Cup was the first international tournament to be held in 12 years. Brazil was the host country, and it built a stadium that could hold 200,000 fans just for the occasion. Brazil was cruising along, crushing one country after another, until it met its teeny, tiny neighbor Uruguay. And on July 16, Uruguay won 2-1, an upset so devastating that every one of the players on the Brazilian team was tainted with it for the rest of his sporting life.

WE CAN'T SEE WHY the story of Michael Chang's match against Ivan Lendl in the 1989 French Open is not printed on cereal

boxes, or made into a movie. The match showed one thing, pure courage, and maybe another, brains. Lendl was the number one player in the world, and entered the fourth set leading 2-1. Now, 17-year-old Chang's legs began to cramp, and the pain grew worse, and worse, and worse. He could barely move on the court, so he would hit the ball high in the air to give himself a moment's rest.

He began screaming in pain as he played, he even served underhand, and finally, he stood completely out of position when Lendl served to break his concentration. Amazingly, Chang, who could hardly stand, won the fourth and fifth sets and the match, then collapsed into tears.

IN 1954, TINY MILAN High School in rural Indiana had only 75 male students. But it had a very determined basketball coach. Marvin Wood molded the team into a unit that had reached the state semifinal the year before. Then came the real run. First, Milan beat an Indianapolis school whose star, Oscar Robertson, was one of the greatest players of all time. Then in a close, low-scoring game for the state title, Milan held the ball with just seconds left. Bobby Plump, who had just missed another big shot, made it with time running out, and the school from nowhere ruled the state. Sports fans voting onlin

...ZING

...REFUSE-TO-LOSE

...alled the movie *Hoosiers,* ...vhich is loosely based on the ...tory of Milan, the greatest ...ports movie of all time.

...N 1869, THERE WAS ...only one all-professional ...aseball team in the world, ...he Cincinnati Redstockings, ...nd their record proved it. ...fficially, the team only went ...7-0 that year, but that was ...ecause the captain didn't ...ount the 20 or so other ...ames it won against teams ...hat were not in the National ...ssociation. The streak kept ...oing in 1870 until it reached ...30 wins (81 against Associa-...ion teams). But on June 14, ...he Brooklyn Atlantics won 8-...in extra innings—about as ...ig an upset as you can get.

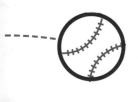

SOMETIMES AN UPSET is so upsetting the loser does not agree to accept the result. Take the finals of the 1972 Olympic Gold Medal

basketball game between the United States and the Soviet Union. America had never lost an Olympic basketball game, but the Soviets led throughout the final game, until, with three seconds left, the Americans went up 50-49. One second left. But wait, the Soviets claim they had asked for time and did not get it. No

ref agrees. But, somehow, the clock is changed; now there are three seconds left. Game starts again. Soviets fail to score. America wins.

Or not. The Soviets again demand their three seconds. Finally with three new seconds, a pass, a shot, a score—the Soviet Union goes up 51-50, defeats the Americans, and wins the gold medal. The American team protests and, to this day, refuses to accept their second-place silver medals.

BEST INDIVIDUAl

BALL GAMES

SPORTSFAN A: The Lakers were sure to lose the sixth game of the 1980 NBA finals to the 76ers. L.A.'s best player, six-time most valuable player Kareem Abdul-Jabbar, was injured and could not play. They had no center to replace him. So the 6-foot-9 rookie Erwin "Magic" Johnson, normally a tall guard, became a small center—and dominated the game. Magic earned his nickname, scoring 42 points, grabbing 15 rebounds, and handing out 7 assists. Single-handedly, Magic made sure L.A. won the game and took the series.

SPORTSFAN B: Good game for Magic, good game. Too bad he scored so few points—compared with Wilt. On the night of March 2, 1962, Wilt Chamberlain of the Philadelphia Warriors scored 100 points against the New York Knicks.

One zero zero. And if you think maybe he just got lucky for one night, that year, he averaged 50 points and 25 rebounds a game. That is just about double what anyone scores or rebounds in the NBA today. Wilt was unstoppable.

SPORTSFAN A: Yeah, Wilt scored a lot, but he also took 63 shots in a meaningless game. His whole team spent the second half feeding him the ball, so he could get to triple digits. In the 1973 NCAA Finals, Bill Walton had it harder.

UCLA needed to win to take their seventh consecutive crown, and to complete an undefeated year. Walton made sure they did, shooting an astonishing 21-22 from the floor, and ensuring another championship. He missed one shot and three foul shots. Otherwise, for

that one night, he was no merely great, he was perfect

SPORTSFAN B: Come or very tall men scoring point is not headline news. Physi cist Robert Adair says tha one of the hardest feats in al sports is to hit a rapidly mov ing sphere with a cylindrica bat. Which brings me to Reg gie Jackson in the 197 World Series. The Dodger had won game five, but a least Reggie hit a home ru in his last at bat.

Game six was back in Nev York, at Yankee Stadium Reggie walked his first tim up. Then he hit three consec utive home runs—on th first pitch to him in the bot tom of the fourth, another o: the first pitch he saw in th fifth, and a third, again o: the first pitch, in the eighth Four home runs in a rov three in one game, one pitc. after another. Impossible, bu true. The Yankees took th game and the series.

SPORTSFAN A: And the we have the Boston Colleg versus Miami football gam on Thanksgiving Day c

---

Six families have had more than one member drafted in the first round of the NFL draft: Ed and Brad Budde; Billy Cannon and Billy Cannon Jr.; Dub and Bert Jones; Steve and Keith DeLong; and then there are the Mannings: Archie was second pick in the 1971 draft, Peyton the first pick in 1998, and Eli was the first pick in 2004.

ᵖERFORMANCE

984. It was not a bowl game, but the whole country was off that day, at home, eating turkey and watching the game. With just 28 seconds eft, Miami capped an amazing 90-yard drive with a ouchdown, giving it a 45-41 ead. BC's 5-foot-9 quarterback, one determined Doug lutie, completed two passes o get to midfield. Then, with en seconds left in the game, e sent all his receivers long nd threw the ball 60 yards ownfield, right into the aiting arms of Gerry Phean—touchdown, BC! A deseration heave is called a ail Mary, and Flutie's pass s the Hail Mary of all Hail Marys.

XTREME SPORTS

E ASKED STEVE CAVE, he skateboard guide for bout.com, for his top five oments in skateboarding istory and his top five tricks o know. Take it away, Steve:

op Five Moments

he Zephyr team shows up at he 1975 Del Mar skateboarding competition and changes kateboarding forever. Before his moment, most people

saw skateboarding as a hobby, something light-hearted. The Zephyr team was made of outcasts and punks who rode low and hard, with a lot of attitude.

In 1978, Alan "Ollie" Gelfand invents the ollie, the foundation of almost all technical skateboarding tricks. Rodney Mullen later tweaks the trick and creates the flatland ollie.

Stacey Peralta and George Powell form the Bones Brigade, the first video skateboarding team and the strongest skateboarding team ever assembled (including Tony Hawk, Rodney Mullen, Lance Mountain, and Steve Caballero).

In 1983, Tony Hawk is the first to land the frontside 540

in competition. Two years later he premieres the 720. Then, in the 1999 X-Games, with the clock ticking he tries once, twice, five times, ten times—by now time has run out—but on his 11th try, he nails a 900—two and a half spins in the air. No one had ever done that in competition, and whether anyone had ever done it at all is matter of dispute and legend.

(Now fans are hoping that the carrot-topped Shaun White—who was trained by Tony Hawk and is as good at snowboarding as skateboarding—will land the 1080, three complete rotations. Shaun took gold in the 2007 Skateboard Vert—no 1080, but still, a nice shiny medal.)

In 2004, Danny Way gets 79 feet in the air—not only taking gold in the first-ever X-Games Big Air contest, but setting a new world record. The next year he's sure to lose, after fracturing his ankle while trying to become the first person in history to leap over the Great Wall of China without an engine. But his fourth jump, a 360 frontside and a floating, arms spread "Christ Air," ends the suspense—Danny is golden.

Top Five Moves

1) The **ollie** is where you slap the tail of your skateboard on the ground and at the same time jump up into the air. It looks like you're jumping, with the board stuck to the soles of your shoes. It takes a lot of practice, but if you can't ollie, you'll be stuck to the ground unless you ride the half pipe, which skateboarders and BMX bikers call vert.

2) The **manual** is a sort of skateboarding wheelie—you balance on your back wheels while rolling along. It's a lot harder than it looks, but the manual is perfect for mixing in with other tricks. After learning to manual, you can learn to nose manual.

3) The **shuvit** is where you jump a little into the air (not an ollie, just a jump), and you spin the board around underneath you before you land. It looks cool, and is actually pretty easy. Once you can shuvit, you can learn to pop shuvit, where you add an ollie into the mix for more air.

4) **Kickflips** are a high ollie, but while you are in the air you kick the board with your foot and flip it over completely, back to the wheels facing the ground before you land on it. Learn to kickflip, and you can branch off to heelflip,

and pressure flips. Stick with t, and you'll be able to pull off a tre flip (360 flip).

) For a **50-50 grind**, skating along, either ollie up onto a rail or ride off onto the edge of a curb or ledge, grinding along on your trucks instead of your wheels. It's the easiest grind to learn, but once you have it dialed in you can go for 5-Os, Crooks, and eventually board slides (for more about these and other moves, check out www.skateboard.about.com).

BMX BEST

James Stewart Jr. may be old—22 is getting up there—but he is really, really good at motocross. How's this: He tried out his first race when he was just four; won more amateur titles than anyone before him; was rookie of the year in 2002 when he turned pro; and was the youngest National Champion in motocross history. They don't call him the Tiger Woods of Motocross for nothing.

DATES

1829

Boy's Own Book describes a game called Round Ball, with a bat, four bases, strikes, and outs.

There are all sorts of claims about where baseball was invented, but people have been throwing balls and hitting them with bats forever—there is a nice drawing of just that in a book made for King Alfonso X of Spain in the 1200s. The question is when all of that fun started to take shape as baseball—and for that, this is a good date.

1869

Rutgers defeats Princeton 6-4 in the first football game. People have been kicking around balls or whatever they could move across a field ever since guys have had free time, but this game—which was closer to rugby than modern football—is where the road to the Super Bowl began.

1891

James Naismith invents basketball in a Springfield, Massachusetts, YMCA.

1893

The first gasoline-powered car in America runs on roads—also in Springfield. The car is designed by Charles and Frank Duryea—maybe they were in a rush to get to a game.

1895

First car race in America, 54 miles from Chicago to Evanston and back. Frank Duryea wins in a car of his own design, averaging 7.3 miles per hour while moving, but he had to stop and wait for four minutes while a long train passed by, and paused for an hour to fix his engine. The second-place car arrived nearly two hours later.

1936

Hank Luisetti unveils his jump shot at New York's Madison Square Garden and leads Stanford to end Long Island University's 43-game winning streak. Hank was not the first to shoot a jump shot, but coaches kept telling players to stop it and keep their feet on the ground, until he proved them wrong.

1939

Little League Baseball begins, in Williamsport, Pennsylvania.

⟩ KNOW

MERICA

⟩omeplace in California, skateboarding is born. No one knows who ⟩tarted it or when, but a lot of people claim to be the first. What we know ⟩r sure is that around then, a lot of surfers started nailing wheels to the ⟩ottoms of wood boxes and planks, and they started trying to surf the side-⟩valks. It was awkward and dangerous, but it was skateboarding.

OK, reader, you're on—find the guy who nailed the first wheel to the ⟩ottom of the first box.)

| | 1950s |

⟩irst televised Little League World Series. **1953**

⟩Villiam Higinbotham invents the first-known video game—Tennis for ⟩wo—at Brookhaven National Labs. **1958**

⟩hicago Roller Skate creates an inline roller skate boot (a later competitor ⟩ called Rollerblade). **1966**

⟩irst Super Bowl—Green Bay over Kansas City 35-10. **1967**

⟩irst Robot Wars held, the South Bay Mauler wins the first contest. **1994**

⟩SPN holds the first X-Games competition, which shoves skateboarding ⟩to the spotlight. Having a big competition like this helped make skate-⟩oarding look more legitimate to the public. **1995**

⟩azuki Takahashi invents Yu-Gi-Oh. **1996**

⟩intendo releases Wii—a game player, not a game. **2006**

P10 C2 L3 4 P13 C1 L4 2 P132 C2 L1 5 P39 C3 L1 1 P107 C1 L11 1
P20 C2 L3 2 P101 C2 L9 5 P62 C2 L6 1 P66 C1 L5 4 P120 C1 L9 5
P107 C2 L34 3 P154 C3 L7 2 P70 C1 L3 2 P107 C2 L4 1

T R E A

BURIED AN

THE MONEY PIT OF OAK ISLAND
NOVA SCOTIA, CANADA

Two hundred years ago, a strange pit was discovered on Oak Island. Those who dug into it found that it was a shaft with layers of planks and logs and underground passages. In the years since, hundreds of men and their companies have tried to dig the pit all the way to the bottom. But at different levels the pit floods with water or collapses in on itself. Despite digging the pit and the surrounding area down to more than 200 feet with modern cranes, no one has been able to find exactly what the pit contains.

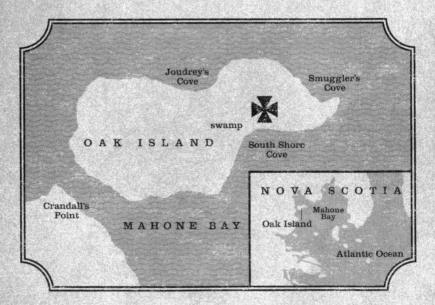

 U ot I dna, O ot G, I ot F, E ot W, A ot stpyrced J: 1G elzzup Naidraug re
Tnih.

SURE
THERWISE

RMS *REPUBLIC*
ATLANTIC OCEAN

In 1909, this ocean liner collided with another ship some 50 miles off the coast of Massachusetts. Six people were killed in the accident, but everyone else was rescued before the *Republic* sank. After it went down, rumors spread that the ship had been carrying gold worth nearly $5 billion (in today's dollars). Treasure hunters finally located the wreck of the ship in 1981, lying upright 270 feet underwater. While numerous divers have attempted to recover the alleged treasure, so far, no one has succeeded.

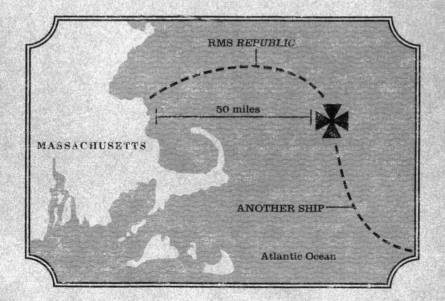

Kxz ntfd dutps tivup 1400 qbq Kufpd L zbf t hbc htvvwu hd asbfc hxzs?

CAPTAIN KIDD'S TREASURE
LONG ISLAND SOUND, NEW YORK AND CONNECTICUT

In 1699, Captain William Kidd buried $30,000 worth of treasure (worth a cool million today) on Gardiners Island off the eastern tip of New York's Long Island. As he was sailing up to Boston to be tried as a pirate, he had to unload his loot, which consisted of gold, silver, coins, and jewels. Kidd paid the island's owner for her trouble, and then went to Boston. But during the trial, the government forced the landowner, Mrs. Gardiner, to hand over the treasure for use as evidence during the trial. Kidd is also alleged to have buried additional treasure on various islands off the coast of Connecticut. Kidd never revealed any other locations where he might have hidden his stolen goods, and he was eventually hanged for his crimes. To this day, the treasure at Gardiners Island is the only instance of a pirate's actual buried treasure ever being found.

 Fubirst hubint fubor thube Ubultubimubate pubuzzuble: Yubou wubill nube uban ubatlubas, ubor thube ubintubernubet.

LONG ISLAND'S SHIPWRECK VALLEY

LONG ISLAND, NEW YORK

On the south shore of Long Island, just a few miles from New York City, more than 400 ships have met their doom from wicked weather and fast-moving currents over the past 300 years. There may be thousands more that have yet to be discovered. With all of those ships sunk into the dark, cold, and fast water of the Atlantic Ocean, it's been estimated that there may be billions of dollars worth of treasure just waiting....

54 61 6B 65 20 74 68 65 20 61 6E 73 77 65 72 20 74 6F 20 47 38 20 61
6E 64 20 6D 75 6C 74 69 70 6C 79 20 69 74 20 62 79 20 47 31 31 2E

THE TOMB OF TUT
THE VALLEY OF THE KINGS, EGYPT

The Valley of the Kings, an area in Egypt where the ancients buried their pharaohs in gold coffins and majestic tombs, was thoroughly explored by 1912. There was nothing left to be found—or so thought many archaeologists. An explorer named Howard Carter didn't believe it; from years of research, he was certain that there must be many more. So he spent 15 years searching for the legendary tomb of Nebkheperure Tutankhamen, known as King Tut. In 1922, digging in a previously excavated area, Carter came upon some steps leading to an undiscovered and secret chamber. He managed to dig a small hole in its doorway, and peered in with the light from a candle. Eager to know what he had found, his fellow archaeologists asked Carter if he could see anything in the darkness. "Yes," he replied. "Wonderful things." When he finally opened the chamber door, Carter uncovered one of the best-preserved tombs in all of Egypt. King Tut's final resting place had been undisturbed for over 3,000 years and was full of ancient treasures—boats, toys, hunting equipment, vases, lamps, and containers for his internal organs—many of them made from gold.

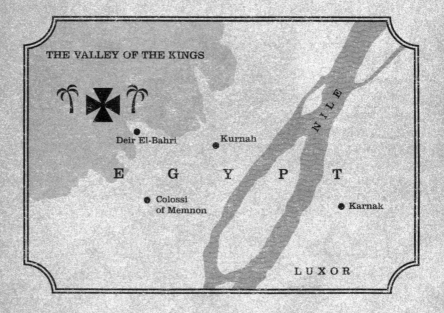

THE VALLEY OF THE KINGS

Deir El-Bahri   Kurnah

E   G   Y   P   T

NILE

Colossi of Memnon   Karnak

LUXOR

LOST DUTCHMAN MINE

APACHE JUNCTION, ARIZONA

Digging for gold in the 1850s, prospector Jacob Waltz (a German mistakenly identified as Dutch) allegedly dug into a significant vein of gold in the Superstition Mountains outside of Phoenix. When he headed into town to claim his new find, he was attacked by strangers and gravely wounded. Jacob made it to a doctor and told him about the mine before dying. But he left no actual map or directions. Since then, people who have looked for the gold mine have a way of ending up dead or disappearing forever. It's said that the mine is cursed, or at least protected by someone who wants it to stay hidden forever.

54 68 65 20 6F 70 70 6F 73 69 74 65 20 73 69 64 65 73 20 6F 66 20 61 20 64 69
65 20 61 64 64 20 75 70 20 74 6F 20 74 68 69 73 20 6E 75 6D 62 65 72 2E

WONDERS O

TWENTY CENTURIES AGO, Greek scholars made a list of the greatest construction proje
ever. Here's a quick tour of the Seven Wonders of the Ancient World.

Fig. A

GREAT PYRAMID OF GIZA, EGYPT, AROUND 2500 B.C. (Fig. A)

More than two million stones, each weighing about as much as a small car, are stacked in four triangles whose points meet nearly 500 feet up into the sky. Scholars estimate that it took 100,000 laborers—mostly slaves from conquered lands—20 years to build the Great Pyramid. They built it so well that it is the only Wonder still standing. For more than 4,000 years, it was the tallest building in the world. In fact, the Great Pyramid was already old by the time the ancient Greeks got around to making this list.

HANGING GARDENS OF BABYLON, IRAQ, 600 B.C.

King Nebuchadnezzar II lived with his queen in the rugged desert outside of Baghdad. When she asked to take a walk through parks and waterfalls, he supposedly built her a mountainside palace with 100-foot-high terraces that supported trees and plants. No one is quite sure what happened to this

glorious creation, and it r have been abandoned c time and simply left to ru

TEMPLE OF ARTEM. TURKEY, 600–300 B.C (Fig. B)

As big as a football field as tall as a five-story buil (according to some), this t ple was built by anci Greeks to honor Artemis, goddess of the hunt (Romans called her Diana) course, no one is quite s exactly how big it w because a band of invac Goths destroyed it in A.D. !

Fig. B

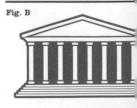

THE WORLD

~~ST~~ATUE OF ZEUS AT ~~OL~~YMPIA, GREECE, 500 ~~B.C~~. (Fig. C)

~~Usi~~ng ivory and gold, the ~~scu~~lptor Phidias created a ~~40-f~~oot-high statue of Zeus ~~seat~~ed on his throne as a ~~mon~~ument to the Olympic ~~Gam~~es. Despite its huge size, ~~the~~ statue eventually disap-~~pea~~red off the earth. Many ~~hist~~orians believe that a fire ~~con~~sumed it.

MAUSOLEUM OF MAUSSOLLOS, HALICARNASSUS, TURKEY, 353 B.C.

When King Maussollos died, his wife brought sculptors and designers from Greece to work on his tomb. They deco-rated the marble building with life-size statues of lions, horses, chariots, and soldiers. An earthquake destroyed Maussollos's tomb, and scav-engers used the crumbled pieces for other buildings. The beauty of the site lives on in ancient writings, and this wonder has also lasted in one unique way: The word "mausoleum" comes from it.

COLOSSUS OF RHODES, GREEK ISLAND OF RHODES, 280 B.C. (Fig. D)

Imagine sailing into a harbor through two giant legs. Leg-end has it that ancient Greek workers crafted a bronze statue of Helios, the god of

Fig D

the sun, so tall that it stood with one foot on either side of Rhodes harbor. Colossus guarded the harbor for more than 50 years until an earth-quake knocked him down in 224 B.C. Later scholars believed he stood 105 feet tall.

LIGHTHOUSE OF ALEXANDRIA, EGYPT, 280 B.C.

Alexandria was one of the busiest ports in the ancient world, so not just any light-house would do. Alexandria's

Sometime around 300 B.C. a Greek explorer named Pytheas sailed from the Mediterranean Sea toward the north. He passed around England—and using his knowledge of the stars, and a kind of sundial, he estimated its size almost as well as we can today with sophisticated instruments. Then he sailed onward through ice and slush, which he reported "binds all together, and can be traveled neither on foot nor by boat." Making his way even in days of nearly total darkness, he probably reached Iceland. And then, having noted all he saw, he sailed back. At the time, many believed he made up the story of his travels. But his descriptions were both specific and accurate.

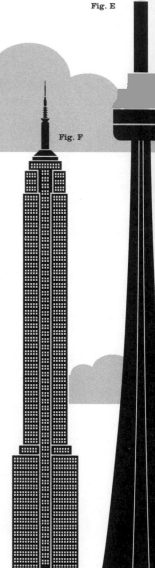

Fig. E

Fig. F

was over 400 feet tall and the keeper always kept a massive fire lit at its top. Storms and earthquakes constantly battered this wonder, which finally fell into the sea during the 1400s.

MA: *Maybe I'd feel differently if I saw them, but the Seven Wonders sound like a lot of large buildings to me. A real ancient wonder: the Antikythera mechanism—a kind of computer for predicting the movements of planets and stars that the Greeks built around 100 B.C. That was amazing.*

OF THESE SEVEN WONDERS, only the pyramids are still standing. Since then, the American Society of Civil Engineers has compiled a list of Seven Wonders of the Modern World, the greatest building achievements of the 20th century.

CHANNEL TUNNEL, STRAIT OF DOVER, ENGLAND, 1994
This 31-mile-long tunnel connects England to France underneath the seabed of the English Channel. It took six and a half years to build, but visionaries dreamed about it for more than a century. You don't walk or drive through it; instead, the widest trains ever built rush through the tunnel at nearly 100 mph. Special ducts are used to release the air that builds up in front of these powerful trains.

CN TOWER, TORONTO (ONTARIO) CANADA, 1976 (Fig. E)
The world's tallest freestanding structure, the CN Tower is 1,815 feet tall. Made of concrete and built in just three years, it weighs as much as 23,214 elephants. Canadian broadcasters use it as a signal tower.

EMPIRE STATE BUILDING, NEW YORK, NEW YORK, 1931 (Fig. F)
It took only one year to build, but when it was finished, the Empire State Building was the world's

est building. It held that
e for 40 years. Plumbers
talled 51 miles of pipe and
ctricians laid 17 million
t of phone wire. But many
inesses were reluctant to
t space in such a high
lding—until the movie
g Kong made it famous
over the world.

LDEN GATE
RIDGE, GOLDEN
TE STRAIT,
N FRANCISCO, CALI-
RNIA, 1937 (Fig. G)

e bridge was designed to
nect the city of San Fran-
o with Marin County. The
ait beneath it is notoriously
gh, which made construc-
extremely difficult. It took
r years to build, requiring
00 miles of cable to make
trong enough to withstand
Francisco's frequent
thquakes. It's been re-
ted that the Golden
te Bridge, because of its
king color and beautiful

setting, is the most pho-
tographed bridge in the world.

ITAIPU DAM,
PARANÁ RIVER,
SOUTH AMERICA, 1984

This dam crosses the seventh-
biggest river in the world, the
Paraná River, which serves as
the boundary between Brazil
and Paraguay. The dam is five
miles wide, and its construction required changing the
course of the river and
enough steel and iron to build
380 Eiffel Towers. It took 14
years to complete.

DELTA WORKS,
NETHERLANDS,
EUROPE, 1997

Because it sits below sea level,
the Netherlands has throughout its history been regularly
damaged by massive floods.
(Have you ever heard the
story of the boy who put his
finger in the dike? It was
based on these floods.) To pre-
vent these disasters, 10,000

miles of dams and dikes were
built over 44 years, making
the Delta Works the biggest
flood control system in the
world. It may also be one of
the most important, as the
Netherlands actually sinks
into the surrounding water at
the rate of about one centime-
ter each year.

PANAMA CANAL,
ISTHMUS OF PANAMA,
CENTRAL AMERICA,
1914

This Central American canal
connects the Atlantic and
Pacific Oceans and allows
ships to pass through without going around South
America. Forty-two thousand
workers spent 34 years working on it, removing enough
dirt and rubble to fill a 16-
foot-wide tunnel to the center
of the earth. More than 5,000
people died during the
canal's construction, many of
them from malaria carried by
mosquitoes.

Fig. G

THE TWO MOST

HORRIFYING,

HIDEOUS,

AND DISGUSTING

CREATURES

IN THE WORLD

THERE ARE LOTS OF SCARY ANIMALS OUT THERE. Bears, tigers, sharks, and cobras can kill you. But the scariest creatures on Earth are not monstrous animals with lots of teeth or venom. Instead, they are tiny little things so hideous that just reading about them can give you the chills. For those of you who want to know just how gross nature can be, welcome the toothpick fish and the guinea worm.

THE TOOTHPICK FISH

The scientific name for this tiny fish is the candiru, and it lives in the Amazon River. It is only a few inches long, needle thin, and has see-through skin so that it is almost invisible in water. The fish is attracted to swimmers and looks for an opening in the body. We're talking about any opening in the body: your mouth, your ear, and even your … Well, you can guess where the other prime places might be.

The fish wriggles into the opening and as soon as it gets comfortable, it shoots a sharp spine into the unwilling victim. This spine locks the candiru into the opening so that there is no way it can be pulled out. Then the fish starts sucking blood out of the victim to use as food. The only way to remove the candiru once it finds its new "home" is through surgery. Unfortunately, there aren't a lot of medical centers deep in the Amazon rain forest, so getting rid of the embedded fish can take a very, very long time.

THE GUINEA WORM

The guinea worm lives in small bodies of water in central Africa. The worm lays its eggs in ponds, where tiny fleas eat them. The fleas are so small that they make it unseen into drinking water. When they get inside your stomach, the fleas dissolve but the worm eggs that they've eaten do not. Instead, the eggs root in your intestines. While there, the worms gradually grow until they are about three feet long. The female worms at this size are filled with new eggs. They need to lay their eggs in water, so they start burrowing through your intestines and organs to get out through your skin.

Once they get just below the skin, and occasionally an eyeball, the worms release an acid that causes your skin to blister and bubble while creating an opening. These blisters are extremely painful, and when you try to wash them with water, the guinea worm bursts out of your body in a long, spaghetti-like strand. You must then grab it and hold on to it. Then, over the course of weeks, you must slowly pull the entire worm out of your flesh, inch by inch, making sure it doesn't break. If it does, the remaining part of the worm could kill you. Since removing it takes so long, the part of the worm already out of the body is wrapped around a stick that you must carry with you until the entire worm wriggles the rest of the way out.

THE GREA

FIRST THING ABOUT PLAYING 21 on a basketball court—be clear on the rules. Depending on where you are in the country, they could be completely different. But the basics are simple:

Rule one: Whoever has the ball is against everyone else—no teams, no passing, no refs, one against all. Call your own fouls, be fair, but the standard is "no harm, no foul."

Rule two: Breaking the Ice—players shoot from the free throw line (or three point line). If you make it, you can try to score; if you miss, the rebounder gets a chance at the line. Unless he has already broken the ice, then he can score at will. (In some places, they skip this stage and go right into the game.)

Rule three: If you make a shot, you get free throws—up to three if you keep making them. If you make all three, you have the ball again and can try to score.

Rule four: If you make a shot, you get two points; a free throw, one point.

Rule five: You must make exactly 21. If you go over, your count goes back to 15 (or 13 or 11).

GAME OF

1

Rule six: If you get a rebound, you have to "take it back" behind the foul line (or the three point line) before shooting.

Rule seven: Air balls or steals you can shoot right away. You don't have to go behind the line first.

Rule eight: If you get to 21, you have to hit a three-pointer from the top of the key, or you go back to 15 (or 13, or 11—except in the parts of the country where you don't have to).

Rule nine: Today, some kids play "tips" or "taps"—tapping a miss right back in (that is, you don't land and shoot, you push the ball back up as it is coming down). The shooter goes back to zero, or 11, or ... In some versions, a one-handed tap takes the shooter to zero, two-handed only to five—there are many variations on this.

Rule ten: MAKE SURE YOU AGREE ON THE RULES.

G5 Elg sthu melyxthdx li irrm enve nx Sm. Rbrarxm? Mer thxgra ml menx pyzzkr nx metm hyswra, snhyx xnq.

FANTASY
WARS

VIKINGS

WARRIORS IN SCANDI-
navia began to go a-viking in
the late 700s—sailing off in
boats whose prows were
meant to look like dragons'
heads, and raiding other parts
of Europe. These relentless
fighters were only stopped by
their own success—by A.D.
1000, many settled in as conquerors. Between the 1500s
and the 1700s, the most
advanced war weapons in the
world were ships that moved
quickly in the wind, and
fired batteries of cannons.
That is why pirates flour-
ished—they controlled the
superweapon of the day. So,
raging Vikings met howling
pirates, who would win?

WHO WOULD WIN?

PIRATES

We called up Dr. John Hale, an expert on Viking longboats. He didn't pause for a second: "Pirates," he said, "no contest." One reason is obvious—better weapons. Pirates had guns and cannons. Vikings had swords and battle-axes. But the other reason takes a moment of thought. Viking boats were low and open— they were for carrying men to battle, not for fighting at sea. Pirate ships were built high and cannons shot from within the boat. Pirates would have shot down at the exposed Vikings and destroyed them with ease.

CRUSHING C

ALEXANDER THE GREAT: They called him Great for a reason—he became king of Macedon (a state north of Greece) in 336 B.C. at the age of 20 when his father, Philip II, was killed, and began fighting at once. Within ten years, he conquered the fractious Greeks, defeated the mighty Persians, took control of Egypt, and swept across what is now Afghanistan and Pakistan. That gave him the largest empire in the entire world at the time. Alexander died at 33—perhaps from illness, though he might have been poisoned—without ever having lost a single battle. He was a brilliant strategist who could size up an enemy, determine where he was weak, and risk everything to exploit that advantage.

GENGHIS KHAN: If you want to know who the greatest conqueror in world history was, look no further. When Genghis died in 1227, he and his fellow Mongols controlled the largest continuous empire the world has ever seen—stretching from the Mediterranean Sea to the Pacific Ocean. The Mongols began training on horseback from childhood, which made them excellent riders, and the composite bow they developed [see page 40] was the ideal weapon to shoot while charging around on a horse. The Mongol Empire no longer exists, but Genghis left a lasting legacy: Genetic tests suggest he is the ancestor of some 16 million people living in Asia today.

HPN: *If Genghis was so great, what happened to his empire and his people? Don't tell me that they hit a wall . . . like the Great Wall of China.*

MA: *A bit like the Vikings (p. 88), the problem with these raider types is that they win. Once a raider conquers a city, he settles in, likes living in a palace, and wants his kids to go to school there. Soon enough, he gets soft, doesn't want to live on horseback and practice archery all day, or try to get past the Great Wall of China. Then the next raider sweeps down and conquers him. That's basically what happened to the Mongol Empire, though Mongolia, the nation, exists to this day.*

JULIUS CAESAR: Now here's a real conqueror. Starting in 58 B.C., Caesar spent eight years fighting in Western Europe. He defeated some 300 tribes, and brought Roman rule north to England and east across Germany—laying the foundations of modern Europe. Caesar had several advantages over the wild Europeans: He could read, and carefully studied to learn how to fight; his men were highly trained and disciplined; and he could befriend anyone while coolly calculating his next move. When pirates captured him, he was relaxed, played dice with them, but told them he would later kill them all, which is just what he did.

After Caesar conquered Europe, he returned to Rome, where by 44 B.C., he was declared dictator, or ruler, having personally changed Rome from a republic to an empire. Not all of the Romans were thrilled with the change; in fact, a group of them got together and stabbed Caesar to death on the floor of the Senate.

FRANCISCO PIZARRO: Winning wars when you have huge armies is fine, but what about when you are outnum-

ᴎNQUERORS

ered—totally outnumbered? n 1532, Pizarro and just 164 men took on and defeated the Inca, who had an 80,000-man army. How come? Just before Pizarro arrived, a smallpox epidemic ravaged the Inca, plunging them into civil war. Still, how would you like to face an army 500 times larger than your own?

PACHAKUTI: Starting in 1438, "Worldshaker," as he called himself, and his sons carved out the largest empire in the world. The Inca Empire ran along the Andes Mountains, stretching from present-day Colombia and Ecuador to Argentina and Chile. The Inca were fearless conquerors with an army of some 250,000 disciplined men, armed with slings, spears, and darts who were known for executing defeated soldiers. An attacking general would make clear to his enemy that to resist was to invite total destruction, so he would encourage his foe to submit without fighting. The Inca's reputation was so powerful that more and more smaller kingdoms accepted their offer. The vast Inca Empire was still growing in 1532

when the Spanish arrived with their horses, guns, and diseases.

EDWARD VII: In 1909, Queen Victoria's son ruled the largest empire in world history. In fact, because of the connections made possible by steamships, railroads, and the telegraph, the British really were the first and only rulers to plant their flag on every continent, from Canada to British Guiana, from India to Australia, from Egypt to South Africa. During Edward's reign, some 20 percent of all people in the world lived in the Empire. But that rule began to unravel five years later, with the beginning of World War I.

NAPOLEON: Alexander conquered enemies who had spears, Genghis ruled a lot of grass, and Pizarro got lucky. If you want a real conqueror, think of Napoleon. Starting in 1796, and facing trained armies with guns, cannons, and horses, he led the French to defeat or control all of Europe from the Atlantic to the eastern edges of Germany. Like Alexander and Caesar, he was brilliant at sizing up his enemy's

strengths and weaknesses (see page 95 for innovative tactics he developed to defeat a larger army). In fact, his most devastating defeat came at the hands of General "Winter"—the cold of Russia, when he tried one invasion too many.

HPN: *You give Napoleon way too much credit. His big claims to fame were some of history's biggest defeats. He marched across Europe to attack Moscow only to find it largely deserted. He lost more than half a million soldiers in the process, mostly to bad weather. And I seem to recall he lost the Battle of Waterloo after saying it would be as easy as eating breakfast. I'll take Genghis any day.*

MA: *Napoleon was one smart guy who made bold and innovative decisions in the heat of battle. I do think that is what makes for a great general. I wonder how he would have done leading the Mongols. How would Genghis have fared if he'd suddenly been put in charge of French soldiers? Hmm . . . reader, what do you think?*

FANTASY
WARS

AZTEC

A SOPHISTICATED CIVI-lization and proud warriors, the Aztec Empire arose in the 1320s in what is now Mexico, and was still growing when Columbus arrived in the Americas. The Inca— masters of the Andes, fabled for their stores of gold— established their first city-state in what is now Peru around 1200; their empire was expanding in 1532. Had the Europeans not arrived, the two great em-pires of the Americas might hav eventually clashed. If the tw powers had met in battl who would have won?

We asked Dr. Ross Ha sig, the world's leading exper

WHO WOULD WIN?

INCA

on Aztec armies. He was clever, and kicked the question back to us: Where, he wondered, would the armies have met? The Aztec didn't use boats to transport armies, and marching to South America from the highlands of Mexico would have taken them through disease-filled jungles. But the Aztec had more men in arms and better weapons. On the other hand, the Inca used rafts with sails, so they could have avoided the jungles and sent an army by sea. Who would have won? Whichever side had planned for the war, knew the other side's strengths, and could bring enough men to fight.

HOW THREE

BEAT FIFT

AND OTHER GREA

OKINAWA ISLAND, 1945
Toward the end of World War II, the United States and its allies brought 548,000 men and 1,300 ships to take an island defended by 100,000 Japanese troops who had spent a year fortifying their positions. The fighting was gruesome in what would become the largest air-sea-land battle of all time. It took a terrible toll on both sides. Some 12,000 Americans were killed, which pales beside the deaths of 107,000 Japanese and an estimated 100,000 natives of Okinawa (the largest island in a chain that makes up the southernmost part of Japan). The grim nature of the battle can be seen in another number: Nearly 38,000 American soldiers sustained physical injuries, and 26,000 suffered from mental stress—they could not face the horror of what was going on around them. In the end, America and its allies won. The bloody fighting is one reason why President Truman agreed to use nuclear weapons on Japan—he did not want more battles that were as devastating as Okinawa.

COSTA RICA, 1856
The shortest battle in histor may have taken place in th Central American nation o Costa Rica. William Walke an American with a wild pla to turn much of Centra America into slave states, ha made himself president o Nicaragua. On March 20 1856, 250 men fighting fo Walker faced a 2,000-ma Costa Rican army determine to stop him. In 15 minutes c fighting, Walker's cre realized they were defeate and ran.

HOUSAND MEN

THOUSAND,

BATTLE STORIES

BENGAL, 1757

On June 23, 1757, Robert Clive and 3,000 English and allied native soldiers faced off against 50,000 French and their allied native warriors near Plassey in Bengal (a region in Southeast Asia). Clive's enemies had the same modern weapons he had, as well as European artillerymen trained to use them. Clive had a river behind him so he could not retreat, and no advantage in terrain. But Clive won the battle. How did he do it?

He bribed the opposing general, offering to make him the ruler of Bengal if he held back his men. The general agreed. Sometimes, knowing how to bend your enemy is more important than trying to break him.

EGYPT, 1798

On July 28th, Napoleon faced an Egyptian army three times his size near the pyramids. The best Egyptian soldiers were cavalrymen, some 4,000 to 6,000 of them. These were professional soldiers who lived for their moments of glory in battle, and they were supported by 40 cannons. But the battle was no contest. Some 2,000 of the horse riders died, against 29 French deaths. How come?

The horsemen only knew how to charge straight ahead. Napoleon formed his men into hollow squares five rows deep. They held their fire until the Egyptians were right in front of them, then picked them off, one by one. According to Dr. Jerome Cormello, a retired colonel and professor of military studies at the U.S. War College, the key to victory was the "organization and discipline" of Napoleon's men, who beat a cavalry whose proud record of victories stretched back to defeating the Mongols in 1303.

FANTASY WARS

MONGOLS

BETWEEN A.D. 1200 AND 1400, no one could take on the Mongols. They were the world's most devastating fighting force. But if you think of grim, unstoppable soldiers, you have to start with the Romans, who built and held their great empire between 57 B.C. and the A.D. 400s. So, what would have happened if these two ruthless conquerors had met in combat?

The Internet is full of debate about this one— often from avid Civilizatio: fans. Most posters agree tha the Mongols had bette weapons. Arrows shot by th exceptional composite bov (see p. 40) they develope

WHO WOULD WIN?

ROMANS

could have pierced Roman shields or armor, and the large, well-organized cavalry would have been too much for Roman soldiers. But fans of Rome don't give up easily— they point out that Mongol victories were short-lived, they blended in with the people they conquered, or gave in to fighting among themselves. Rome's influence lasted for thousands of years. The Romans were also very good at learning from history. If they fought the Mongols and lost, they might well have come back to win another day.

HOW DOES IT WORK?

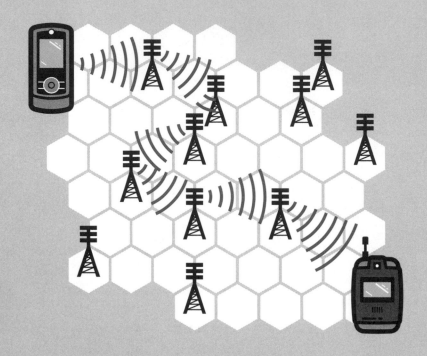

CELL PHONES

HOW DO CELL PHONES WORK? Basically, they're like two-way radios or powerful walkie-talkies. You speak into the phone, and a microphone takes the air vibrations from your mouth and converts them to electrical signals. Those signals are sent into the air. The nearest phone tower picks up your signal and sends it across a network made up of the regular wired phone network and other towers. Your call makes its way through this network in just a few seconds until it finds the person you're calling. Their cell phone receives your electrical signals and reconverts them into voice tones for their earpiece. When they talk back to you, the process is repeated.

Towers act like antennas and help you make the first connection. Most cell phones can send out electrical signals to towers several miles away. But if you're too far from a cell tower, then you can't get reception or your call breaks up.

By the way, the reason they're called "cell" phones is that every tower is considered one cell that is part of a larger group of cells, known as a "cellular network."

Cell phones were invented in 1973, and back then, they weighed almost as much as a brick.

COMPUTER BYTE SIZES

WHEN YOU TALK ABOUT YOUR COMPUT-er's memory or the size of computer files, you probably mention "megs." This is short for "megabytes" or a million bytes. A byte is a computer programming word that refers to a specific amount of information. One byte is just about equal to one letter or one number.

This table shows you how many bytes are in a computer.

Prefix	Bytes
kilo (K)	1,024
mega (M)	1,048,576
giga (G)	1,073,741,824
tera	1,099,511,627,776
peta	1,125,899,906,842,624
exa	1,152,921,504,606,846,976
zetta	1,180,591,620,717,411,303,424
yotta	1,208,925,819,614,629,174,706,176

When computers were built in the 1950s, they were so big that they were stored in rooms the size of a school cafeteria. But they were only as powerful as today's pocket calculators, and they could only handle a few bytes at a time. By the 1980s, most computer memory was measured in kilobytes, which seemed like a lot at the time. In the 1990s, it reached megabytes. Today, we talk more and more about gigabytes. In the next few years, you'll be hearing a lot about petabytes.

Here's how all those numbers translate into familiar paper versions.

1 byte	One letter
10 bytes	Two words
100 bytes	One long sentence
1 KB	Two paragraphs
10 KB	One page in a dictionary
100 KB	A 3 x 5 photograph
1 MB	A 250-page book
10 MB	Two copies of the complete works of Shakespeare, or two songs (MP3s)
100 MB	1 shelf of books four feet long
1 GB	An SUV filled with books
100 GB	The books on one floor of a local public library
1 TB	The paper from 50,000 trees
10 TB	All the books and letters in the U.S. Library of Congress

It is estimated that all the printed paper created every year would equal about 2 exabytes. Another estimate is that we could store a recording of everything ever said by anybody in the history of the world in 42 zettabytes. Not that we'd want to listen to all those people all over again, but it's nice to know that we have the power.

SO YOU WA

ROCK

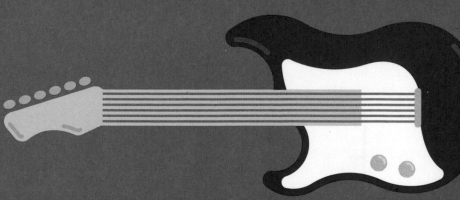

NT TO BE A

STAR

SICIANS MAKE MOST OF THEIR BIG
ney from playing concerts. U2's most
ent concert tour was one of the biggest
istory, bringing in almost $400 million
n ticket sales. Much of that money was
d to pay for crew and transportation
ing the tour.

To get the band set up and on stage every
ht took 16 tractor-trailer trucks, six
es, and 80 crew members—plus a private
This was for the stage, guitars, drums,

microphones, amplifiers, lights, video screens,
and the computers to control it all. Even
with all of this equipment, the average time
to load up the trucks was only two hours.
Over the course of a year and a half, the
band visited five continents, played 132 sold-
out shows, and sold 4,619,021 tickets.

U2 is among a select group of musicians
that make millions of dollars each year. Here
is a list of what the Top 10 moneymaking
musicians made in one year.

U2, $154.2 MILLION

The most popular rock band in the world is U2. They've been performing together since they were all in high school. U2's lead singer, Bono, is well-known for his work in trying to help poor countries in Africa.

THE ROLLING STONES, $92.5 MILLION

The Stones were formed in 1962, more than 45 years ago. The members of the band are all in their sixties, and still perform huge concerts all over the world.

PAUL MCCARTNEY, $56 MILLION

Sir Paul, as he is known, was one of the four Beatles. He was knighted by the Queen of England and is the richest musician in history.

DAVE MATTHEWS BAND, $39.6 MILLION

Matthews was born in South Africa and moved to Virginia as a child. He started his popular band with local musicians, and they have become a popular concert attraction all over the world. He uses some of his money to support farmers and organic crops across America.

GREEN DAY, $31 MILLION

The three members of Green Day have won numerous awards for their punk-style music. They started a charity with U2 to help buy musical instruments for kids whose inst[ru]ments were destroyed by Hurricane Katri[na]

COLDPLAY, $30.1 MILLION

Often compared to U2, Coldplay is one of E[ng]land's most popular bands. They are known supporting many political causes, and clai[m] give 10 percent of all their earnings to cha[rity]

DESTINY'S CHILD, $24.8 MILLION

Destiny's Child is the most popular "[girl] group" of all time, selling more than 50 mil[lion] albums. The three ladies in this band h[ave] each been successful with solo records and [act]ing on Broadway or in movies.

P-DIDDY, $24.3 MILLION

Known by lots of names (Puffy, Puff Da[ddy,] Diddy), Sean Combs not only records album[s] is a successful clothing designer. He also ow[ns a] record company and several restaurants.

GWEN STEFANI, $23.9 MILLION

A longtime member of the band No Do[ubt,] Gwen became even more popular when [she] released solo albums. She has a popular cl[oth]ing line and has also begun an acting care[er.]

50 CENT, $19.7 MILLION

This rapper, born Curtis James Jackson [,] came from a poor family and worked his [way] to become one of the most popular rappers ll time. He has written several books and now appearing in movies.

LLING A LOT OF RECORDS IS ALSO d for a musician's piggy bank. Most musi- ns make about one dollar for every CD d. Here are the 10 musicians who've sold most records in the United States—ever.

THE BEATLES: 168,500,000

e Beatles have sold more than 160 million ums in the U.S., which averages out to more n half the people in this country owning a atles record. They changed history with ir pop music and long haircuts, but only orded for eight years, from 1962 to 1970. ey are still considered the most popular sic group of all time. The Beatles' song "Yes- day" is reportedly the second-most recorded g ever ... after "Happy Birthday to You."

ELVIS PRESLEY: 118,500,000

ring the 1950s and 1960s, this shy young ck driver from Tennessee became the most ular solo artist of all time. He is still called e King of Rock and Roll."

GARTH BROOKS: 116,000,000

aring his black hat wherever he goes, Garth oks is country music's all-time best-selling former. After setting concert attendance rds in the 1990s, he went into semiretire- nt to spend time with his family and work h charities.

LED ZEPPELIN: 109,500,000

s British band was famous for creating d and exciting rock music in the 1970s, but y also recorded many unusual and exotic gs. Zeppelin's "Stairway to Heaven" has n the single most popular song on music io stations for more than twenty years.

5. THE EAGLES: 91,000,000

An American group that performed during the 1970s, the Eagles broke up after band mem- bers started getting into fights with each other. Years later, they reunited and their greatest hits album became the all-time best- selling record in the United States.

6. BILLY JOEL: 79,500,000

A piano player from New York, Joel's songs about life in American towns made him a favorite of radio stations during the 1970s and 1980s. He still tours today, often with Elton John.

7. PINK FLOYD: 73,500,000

This group from London was known for their experimental work with sound and synthesiz- ers during the 1960s and 1970s. Their album *Dark Side of the Moon* spent 741 weeks on the best-seller list, longer than any other recorded piece of music in history.

8. BARBRA STREISAND: 71,000,000

A girl from Brooklyn who suffered from stage fright, Barbra is the best-selling female artist of all time. She is also a successful theater and movie actress and director.

9. ELTON JOHN: 69,000,000

A British pianist whose birth name was Regi- nald Dwight, Elton John became known for his pop songs and flamboyant stage costumes dur- ing the 1970s and 1980s. He is actively involved in many charities and often tours the world with fellow piano man Billy Joel.

10. AC/DC: 66,000,000

Started by two brothers in Australia in the 1970s, AC/DC continues to make records more than 30 years later. Their music and stage cos- tumes provided inspiration for the movie *School of Rock*.

THE ONLY FOUR

SPORTS DYNASTIES

WORTH MENTIONING,

AND WHY NO ONE WILL
EVER TOP THEM

MARCH MADNESS: Since the NCAA tournament began in 1939, only seven teams have ever repeated as champions. Before Florida did it in 2006–07, Duke was the last to defend its title, in 1991–92. Only one has done better than that—much better. UCLA was the NCAA champion in 1964–65. They lost in '66, and then got serious, winning seven times in a row. They lost in 1974, but won again in '75—10 championships in 12 years. No team has ever, or will ever, come close to that record. Coach John Wooden set an example in seeing talent, not race, and crushed teams stuck in the past. Other teams at the time also had black players, but limited how many would play, or treated them as outsiders. Wooden set high standards and treated all his players as equals.

WHO IS THE GREATEST basketball coach of all time? Arnold "Red" Auerbach of the Boston Celtics, no doubt about it. He led the Celtics to the NBA Finals every single year between 1957 and 1966, when he stepped down

as manager; and each time they won, except in 1958. Nine championships in 10 years!

In 1956, Auerbach made a key trade that gave him three top draft picks. He selected Bill Russell and K.C. Jones, two black players who had led San Francisco to consecutive NCAA championships. Auerbach was a pioneer in using any combination of players that would win, and not paying any attention to their race. His disciplined, unselfish champions expected to win, and they did. Due to his legacy, the Celtics have dominated their sport like no other professional team, winning over 26% of all NBA championships. Truth to tell, though, they have not won much in recent years, so that percentage is declining fast.

GO, RED BIRDS! The Saint Louis Cardinals have won 10 World Series. The Boston Red Sox have done well, too, with their six championships—that puts them only 2 behind the New York Yankees. Think of the fabled "Murderer's Row" of the '20s, including Babe Ruth, Lou Gehrig, Tony Lazzeri, and Bob

Meusel. Read about the home-run derbies of Mickey Mantle and Roger Maris. For fun, get a book on the dramatics (members of the team often squabbled with each other) of Reggie Jackson and Ron Guidry. Hunt around on the Web for stories of the efficiency of Derek Jeter and Mariano Rivera. Any place you look, you will see the same story: The Yankees win. All told, Yankee teams have won a full quarter of all the World Series ever held.

HOCKEY CHAMPIONSHIPS come in bunches: Wayne Gretzky and the Edmonton Oilers took the Stanley Cup in 1990, 1988, and '87, as well as 1985 and '84, and they broke the streak of four in a row won by the New York Islanders between 1980 and '83. But the real champion of champions is the Montreal Canadians, who won four in a row before the Islanders' reign, and five in a row between 1956 and '59. In fact, if any team can challenge the Celtics and Yankees as dominant in their sport, it is the Habs (short for *habitant*, French for a farmer from Quebec, the Canadian province in which Montreal is located)—who have won 24 Stanley Cups, just over a quarter of all the hockey championships.

WHY DON'T WE HAVE sports dynasties today? Three simple reasons—free agency, expansion, and the draft. In the old days, players were tied to the team that paid them. The team could trade a player, but a player could not sign with a new team. So, teams stayed together for a long time. Today, expiring contracts cause teams to reshuffle not only every year, but even during a season. A team going nowhere with an expensive player who will leave next year will try to trade him before the year runs out. When the Celtics and Canadians dominated their sports, they had very few rivals. The National Hockey League, for example, had just six teams during much of its early history, until it doubled to twelve in 1967–68. And then there is the draft: Teams with the worst records now get first crack at the best high school and college players. That does not guarantee a team will turn around, but it does mean new stars are spread around.

MAJOR LEAGUE BROTHERS

VINCE, JOE, AND DOM DIMAGGIO all played in the major leagues—with Dom's lifetime .298 average being quite good, and Joe's .325 making him a frequent choice as the best ever.

Felipe, Matty, and Jesus Alou were the first brothers to bat one after another in order. They did it on September 10, 1963. Playing for the San Francisco Giants against the New York Mets—they went down one, two, three. Five days later, they formed the first all-brothers starting outfield in baseball history. Moises, Felipe's son, is still playing, and collectively, the four Alous have played more innings than any other baseball family.

The winningest duo of brother pitchers is Phil and Joe Niekro. Phil's knuckleball won him 318 games in 24 years, and in 22 years, Joe won another 221. Their family total of 539 gives them 10 more than Gaylord and Jim Perry. Joe's son Lance is a first baseman, not a pitcher, but he is playing today.

LARGEST

SPORTS FACILITIES

IN THE UNITED STATES

WHEN YOU WATCH SPORTS ON TV, there are usually thousands of people in the stands, a lot of them screaming their lungs out. But one place dwarfs all those stadiums, and the action is louder than the fans. That's the Indianapolis Speedway during the Indianapolis 500 race. The largest sports facility in history, the Speedway packs in 255,000 people during the race, making it—for one day, at least—one of America's 100 largest cities. The Speedway is so huge that the Kentucky Derby track, Yankee Stadium, the Rose Bowl, Wimbledon's tennis courts, the Roman Coliseum, and Vatican City could all easily fit into the Speedway at the same time.

The main attraction at the Speedway is its track: a 2.5-mile oval designed for high speeds. Cars get so hot during the race that their tires reach 212° Fahrenheit, almost the temperature of boiling water. And they are tremendously loud. Each of the Indy race cars emits about 120 decibels, roughly the same amount of noise that a jet makes.

The only two U.S. stadiums that even come close in size are Michigan Stadium, home of the Michigan Wolverines, which holds 107,501—less than half the total of the Speedway—and FedEx Field, home of the Washington Redskins, which seats 91,665.

A2   Notz lux Magxjogt vaffrk M5: Ayk g yahyzozazout iovnkx, cozn qke kwagr zu ZCUJXOBKTPIQYNRVLGDSEHMWAF.

THE MOST SUCCESSFUL MOVIES EVER SHOWN IN AMERICA

BIG MOVIES ARE BIG EVENTS THAT make actors big stars. But what defines a "big movie"? One word: money. The more money a movie makes, the bigger a blockbuster it is. In Hollywood, it doesn't even matter if you think the movie is great or boring. It just matters that a lot of people pay to see it.

This is how much money these movies made from people actually going to the theater to see them. It doesn't count all the extra millions of dollars that came from DVD or video sales.

1. *Titanic* (1997) $600,779,824

2. *Star Wars* (1977) $460,935,665

3. *Shrek 2* (2004) $436,471,036

4. *E.T.—The Extra-Terrestrial* (1982) $434,949,459

5. *Star Wars: Episode I— The Phantom Menace* (1999) $431,065,444

6. *Pirates of the Caribbean: Dead Man's Chest* (2006) $423,032,628

7. *Spider-Man* (2002) $403,706,375

8. *Star Wars: Episode III— Revenge of the Sith* (2005) $380,262,555

9. *The Lord of the Rings: The Return of the King* (2003) $377,019,252

10. *Spider-Man 2* (2004) $373,377,893

But it also costs a lot to make a movie and advertise it. Let's take *Pirates of the Caribbean: Dead Man's Chest*. It made about $425 million in theaters. That's nearly half a billion dollars. Who got it all?

Theaters took about one-third of all the ticket sales and kept it for themselves. That's about $120 million. So the moviemakers made about $305 million, right? Not quite. With all of its special effects, shipbuilding, filming around the world, the hundreds of workers, and actors' salaries (Johnny Depp made $20 million for starring as Jack Sparrow), the cost to make the film was $225 million. That brings the American total down to $80 million, not counting all the advertisements on TV, radio, magazines, newspapers, and the Internet. For a big movie like *Pirates*, advertising can be almost $50 million. That brings the total down to $30 million.

There's more. It costs about $1,500 to make individual copies of a movie and send it out to the theaters. *Pirates* was shown on more than 8,500 screens when it was released. That adds up to almost $13 million. Now *Pirates* is down to about $17 million. That gets split between all the companies that produced the movie and the banks that helped pay for it.

The big companies all get a few million dollars, and hope that their next movie is as big as *Pirates*. Which is why there are so many sequels: If you went to see the first movie, you'll probably pay to go see the next one, right? That's why all of the biggest blockbusters, except for *Titanic* and *E.T.*, are part of a series or are sequels. Makes you wonder what the next big sequel will be, doesn't it?

HOW TO

CREATE A BLOCKBUSTER MOVIE

SOME OF THE MOST POPULAR MOVIES of all time have each used exactly the same formula to get you interested, excited, and coming back for more. In fact, the formula is something of a secret, but we're going to share it with you.

Take a lead character who is missing one or both parents. Add a sidekick (preferably two), and throw in a very nasty villain—who usually has nasty helpers of his own. Now add a wise individual who understands the ways of the world, and top it off with a potential girlfriend. Hard to believe it's that easy, right? Well, check this out. Now you can write your own movie.

As you can tell from the next page, this works especially well for Disney movies and superheroes. Here's one more secret: This formula was identified by a man named Joseph Campbell, who traced it all the way back to ancient mythology.

Want to know another trick? Read just about any folktale (works best if it's European), or your little brother's picture-book version of a folktale, and there will always be three challenges—for Goldilocks the porridge is too hot, too cold, and just right; for the Three Little Pigs, one builds a house out of straw, one out of sticks, and the smart third one uses bricks; for, well—see if you can find any exceptions and tell us. One hint, look for a culture that is not so interested in the number three, and you might have to search to the four corners of the world.

MOVIE	HERO	SIDEKICK(S)	VILLAIN
Aladdin	*Aladdin*	*Abu*	*Jafar*
Batman	*Bruce Wayne*	*Robin*	*The Joker*
A Bug's Life	*Flik*	*Slim, Heimlich, Dot*	*Hopper*
Cars	*Lightning McQueen*	*Mater*	*Chick Hic*
Harry Potter	*Harry Potter*	*Hermione, Ron*	*Voldemor*
Hercules	*Hercules*	*Pegasus*	*Hades*
The Jungle Book	*Mowgli*	*Baloo*	*Shere Kh*
The Lion King	*Simba*	*Timon, Pumba*	*Scar*
Lord of the Rings	*Frodo*	*Sam, Pippin, Merry*	*Sauron*
Pinocchio	*Pinocchio*	*Jiminy Cricket*	*Stromboli*
Shrek	*Shrek*	*Donkey, Puss*	*Prince Che*
Spider-Man	*Peter Parker*	*Harry Osbourne*	*Green Gol*
Star Wars	*Luke Skywalker*	*R2-D2, C-3PO*	*Darth Vae*
Superman	*Kal-El/Clark Kent*	*Jimmy Olsen*	*Lex Luth*
Tarzan	*Tarzan*	*Tantor, Terk*	*Mr. Clayto*

A15   Gsqcbr vwbh tcf hvs Aoghsf dinnzsg: Wb kvoh gwns fsqhobuzsg kwzz hvs zshh twh dsftsqhzm?

NASTY HELPERS	WISE PERSON	POSSIBLE GIRLFRIEND
ago	*The Genie*	*Jasmine*
enchmen	*Alfred*	*Vicki Vale*
olt	*Queen*	*Atta*
it crew	*Doc Hudson*	*Sally*
ementors	*Dumbledore*	*Cho Chang*
ain, Panic	*Phil*	*Meg*
aa	*Bagheera*	*Shanti*
yenas	*Rafiki*	*Nala*
aruman	*Gandalf*	*None*
onest John, Gideon	*Blue Fairy*	*None*
aptain Hook, Cyclops	*Queen Lillian*	*Fiona*
one	*Aunt May*	*Mary Jane Watson*
tormtroopers	*Obi-Wan Kenobi*	*Princess Leia*
enchmen	*Jor-El*	*Lois Lane*
unters	*Kala*	*Jane Porter*

Int-hay or-fay Uardian-gay uzzle-pay G2: One-way of-way e-thay ords-way is-way
Iekro-nay, and-way e-thay ast-lay ord-way is-way eventy-say even-say.

DATES

MEDIA

1893–1895	Intrepid inventors including Nikola Tesla (U.S., 1893), Oliver Lodge (U.K. 1894), Jagdish Chandra Bose (Calcutta, 1894), Alexander Popov (Russia 1894), and Guglielmo Marconi (Italy, 1895) all experiment with radio. Arguments have raged ever since over who did what first.
1893	Thomas Edison opens the first studio to make movies.
1906	An earthquake and subsequent fire in San Francisco result in some 3,000 deaths—films are made of the event.
1911	The first movie studio in Hollywood opens.
1918	*Cupid Angling,* the first feature silent film in color, is released.
1920	KDKA in Pittsburgh is the first radio station in America.
1928	Philo T. Farnsworth gives the first demonstration of television, which he has been developing since he was a teenager.
1928	*Lights of New York,* the first movie with a complete sound track, opens.
1935	*Becky Sharp,* the first feature film to use three colors, is released.
1954	RCA puts the CT-100, the first color television, on sale.
1960	The number of television sets in America has risen from 6 million in 1950 to 60 million.

Hubint fubor Guubardubiuban pubuzzuble G3: Hubow cubould yubou mubake thubi subentubence thube kubey tubo uba sububstubitubutiubon cubiphuber? Brubight vubixubens jubump; dubozuby fubowl quuback.

) KNOW

MERICA

ernando Corbato sends the first e-mail within a shared computer system.	**1965**
RPANET (Advanced Research Projects Agency Network), a long-distance omputer network that will become the Internet, is launched.	**1966**
ay Tomlinson sends the first e-mail between computers.	**1971**
r. Martin Cooper makes the first call on a portable cell phone.	**1973**
he first desktop personal computer is introduced.	**1974**
he first CDs are sold in America.	**1983**
our young Israelis invent ICQ, which will become instant messaging.	**1996**
he term "blog," first used for weblog, or diary page kept on the Web, s introduced.	**1999**
inety-eight percent of American households have remote-control elevision.	**2000**
pple brings out the iPod.	**2001**
lectronic Arts releases the video game Spore.	**2007**

Jhh rbw jdsuwos rg X-sfy jdh X-pfprwwd rg xwr rbw jdsuwo rg rbfs ciqqkw.

EARTH'S EXTREMES

THE HIGHEST POINT on the Earth's surface is Sagarmatha (Nepalese for "head of the sky"), also known as Mount Everest, which is located on the border of Nepal and Tibet. The top of the mountain is 29,028 feet above sea level. More than 2,000 people have climbed it, but one out of every ten dies. English explorer Sir Edmund Hillary and his Tibetan guide Norgay made the first successful summit of Mount Everest, without a map and without a path to follow. In 1953, they didn't have cell phones or special jackets, unlike today's climbers, who almost always use modern technology. They were just intent on climbing up 29,035 feet—almost five and a half miles into the sky—and doing it together.

THE LOWEST POINT on the Earth's surface is the Marianas Trench, located in the Pacific Ocean between Japan and Indonesia. Its deepest point is 35,798 feet below sea level. Only two people have made it all the way down. Jacques Piccard and Don Walsh piloted a small submarine just 50 feet long called the *Trieste* to the bottom of the ocean—and

below. They entered a section of the Marianas Trench known as the Challenger Deep, which took them all the way down to the bottom. That's nearly seven miles straight down into the water, and the pressure is eight tons per square inch (equal to four cars standing on top of one postage stamp). No one has ever gone deeper since that amazing day in 1960.

THE HOTTEST SPOT on Earth is Al Azizyah in Libya, Africa. On September 13, 1922, it recorded the hottest outdoor temperature ever measured: 136° Fahrenheit (57.8° Celsius). Located on the northern edge of the Sahara Desert, Libya is considered one of the hottest countries in the world. Many of its inhabitants travel across the desert land as nomads, living in tents and searching for food and water. And, presumably, trying to get out of the heat.

THE COLDEST SPOT on Earth is Antarctica. On July 21, 1983, at the outpost of Vostok, scientists recorded the coldest outdoor temperature ever measured: -129° Fahrenheit (-89° Celsius). Vostok is uninhabited, except

for the occasional brave researcher.

THE DRIEST PLACE on Earth is Arica, Chile, which gets a fraction of an inch of rain—3/100ths of an inch actually—every year. That means it would take 30 years to get an inch of water. Its dryness is so unusual because the city is a beach town sitting on the Pacific Ocean.

THE WETTEST PLACE on Earth is Lloro, Colombia, which gets an average of 40 feet of rain a year (523.6 inches, to be exact). The locals make their living from chopping down the trees in the town's "cloud forest," where it rains just about every day.

THE TEMPERATURE OF THE EARTH gets hotter as you go deeper and deeper into the ground. The center of the Earth is 4,000 miles straight down and estimated to have a temperature close to 9,000° Fahrenheit. Scientists have figured this out using computer models of how much pressure must be built up at the Earth's core. They use these models to calculate how hot the core must be, although no one has ever drilled down more than 7.5 miles.

THE HIGHEST POINT

MOUNT EVEREST
Located on the border of Nepal and Tibet

THE LOWEST POINT

MARIANAS TRENCH
Located in the Pacific Ocean between Japan and Indonesia

THE HOTTEST SPOT

AL AZIZYAH
Located in Libya, Africa

THE COLDEST SPOT

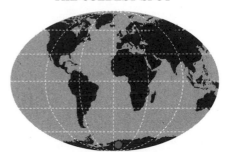

ANTARCTICA

THE DRIEST PLACE

ARICA, CHILE
Located in South America

THE WETTEST PLACE

LLORO, COLOMBIA
Located in South America

Cx anjm Pdjamrjw ydiiun P15, dbn FJUCIKMWHVYQOXAZDRLTSPBENG jb cqn tnh cx j bdkbcrcdcrxw lryqna.

MOON MAN

BEFORE NEIL ARMSTRONG PUT HIS FOOT on the silent surface of the moon, no man had ever stepped anywhere outside of Earth. But Neil and his partner Edwin "Buzz" Aldrin set down on a place that the rest of us only see up in the sky. The third member of the mission, Michael Collins, piloted their return craft. Nobody knew if it would work, but they made it—one of the great achievements in all of history.

Each NASA *Apollo* spacecraft had three crew members. Two of those members descended to the moon in the Lunar Module, while o stayed behind to control the Command M ule. In all, six of these missions made it to moon. And each visit to the moon had sor thing a little different about it, thanks to men who walked on it.

1. *Apollo 11* (1969) Neil Armstrong and Edv "Buzz" Aldrin
There are no solo photos of Neil Armstro on the moon because the plan to take picture was interrupted by a surprise from President Richard Nixon.

FACTS

Apollo 12 (1969) Charles "Pete" Conrad and Alan Bean

Bean left a banner from his high school, Paschal High in Texas, on the moon.

Apollo 14 (1971) Alan Shepard and Edgar Mitchell

Shepard was the only man to ever play golf on the moon. He said his golf ball soared for "miles and miles."

Apollo 15 (1971) David Scott and James Irwin

Irwin developed heart trouble on the mis-sion, but the zero gravity of the moon and the pure oxygen in his suit kept his heart working just fine.

5. *Apollo 16* (1972) John Young and Charles Duke

These two astronauts spent the most amount of time on the moon: 3 days.

6. *Apollo 17* (1972) Gene Cernan and Harrison Schmitt

These two were the "last men on the moon," and drove 22 miles over its surface in a specially built Lunar Rover.

ROAD TO THE RED PLANET

NASA's next set of flights to Mars are all designed to place machines on the Red Planet. All of the knowledge they gain will help prepare for the big day when humans finally reach another planet.

SCHEDULED DEPARTURE	VEHICLE	PURPOSE
Spring 2007	Phoenix	Look for water
Fall 2009	Martian Space Lab	Check for chemical building blocks of life
Not yet set	Still being planned	Bring back rocks
Not yet set	Still being planned	Drill beneath Martian soil
2016	A very expensive machine; the Mars trip will probably have a flight crew from more than one rich nation.	Human contact

S P A C E   D

SPACE IS NOT THAT FAR. It's just under 300 miles away, or the distance from Phoenix to Los Angeles, or from Pittsburgh to Philadelphia. Sure, you have to go through a few layers of atmosphere to get there, but it's pretty close. After that, however, the distances get really extreme. Here's what you have to get through to reach space.

Troposphere (Fig. A): from ground level up to 12 miles. This is where clouds and almost all the water vapor over Earth exist. Mt. Everest reaches almost halfway up through it.

Stratosphere (Fig. B): 12 miles to 30 miles up. The stratosphere absorbs a lot of the sun's radiation, so a lot of chemical reactions occur in this layer. It is also where the ozone layer exists.

Mesosphere (Fig. C): from 30 miles to 50 miles up. Here's where heat begins to completely disappear from the atmosphere. Many gases are trapped in this layer, which is where objects hitting the atmosphere tend to burn up. Clouds made of ice also exist here.

Thermosphere (Fig. D): from 50 to about 250 miles up. This is where space starts turning black because there aren't enough molecules to scatter light. Atoms are so far apart that they can become electrically charged by the sun's radiation, and radio waves from some broadcasts are bounced off them so that they will travel beyond the horizon. The space shuttle and lower-Earth orbit satellites operate here, at about the 103-mile mark.

Exosphere (Fig. E): from 250 miles on to the rest of the universe. Space starts here, the last part of the atmosphere where molecules and gases can leave Earth. Space is thought of as a vacuum where atoms are spread out so far that they don't form molecules of anything— although in reality, some gases still exist in space.

Satellite band: 22,300 miles up. This is the orbit in which satellites can hold a fixed position above a specific point. At this height, a satellite is traveling at the same speed at which the Earth rotates because it is at the far edge of our planet's gravitational pull. Most satellites are placed in this geosta-

tionary orbit, meaning they stay fixed above one particular point on the Earth all the time. At 22,300 miles up, temperatures are at absolute zero (-459° Fahrenheit).

Astronomers measure distance in space by light-years because miles are too small. It would be like trying to measure the United States in inches. Would you rather say 190,080,000 inches or 3,000 miles? A light-year equals 5.88 million million miles (a trillion miles), and is the distance light travels in one year, at the speed of 186,282 miles per second. Some good space distances to know are:

Moon (Fig. F): 238,854 miles away. It's the closest object in the solar system to Earth.

Mars (Fig. G): 36,000,000 miles away (at its closest). It's our nearest planetary neighbor.

Sun (Fig. H): 93,000,000 miles away. It takes about eight minutes for light from the sun to reach Earth. That means that if something happened on the sun right this second, we wouldn't see it for another eight minutes.

S T A N C E S

Proxima Centauri (Fig. I): This is the nearest star to our sun; it is 4.3 light-years away.

The distances in space are hard for us to imagine. So try this: Let's make the sun the size of a volleyball. If it were this small, then Earth would be the size of a pinhead and Jupiter, the largest planet, would be as big as a marble. At this size, our Milky Way Galaxy is about the size of a huge shopping mall and its parking lot, with the volleyball and pinhead and marble sitting on the ground next to one another. And even at this size, Proxima Centauri is still 4,000 miles away. That means if our shopping mall galaxy were located in New York, our nearest neighbor would be in Rome, Italy.

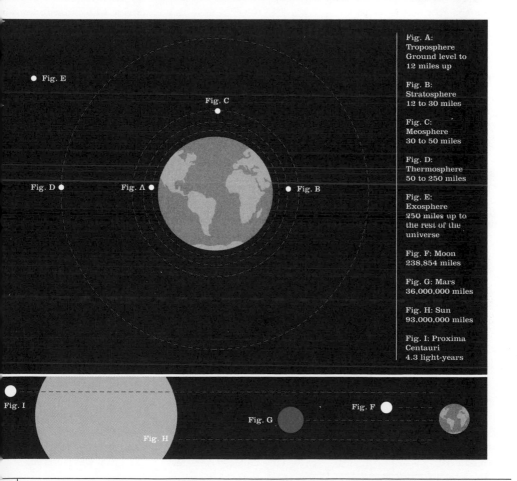

Fig. A:
Troposphere
Ground level to
12 miles up

Fig. B:
Stratosphere
12 to 30 miles

Fig. C:
Meosphere
30 to 50 miles

Fig. D:
Thermosphere
50 to 250 miles

Fig. E:
Exosphere
250 miles up to
the rest of the
universe

Fig. F: Moon
238,854 miles

Fig. G: Mars
36,000,000 miles

Fig. H: Sun
93,000,000 miles

Fig. I: Proxima
Centauri
4.3 light-years

16   Tcifhv usbsfoz vwbh: Kvoh wg hvs Oasfwqob Ghobrofr Qcrs tcf Wbtcfaohwcb
      Wbhsfqvobus (OGQWW)?

COOL THINGS TO EXPECT
IN YOUR LIFETIME

Invisibility cloak. There's nothing magic to this because it won't really make you invisible. Instead, a small camera on the neck of the cloak will send images of what is directly behind you to the front of the cloak, which acts as a type of computer or movie screen. The person looking at you will see what's behind you, making it appear as if you're not there. Scientists have already developed simple versions of this cloak and call it "optical camouflage."

Flying cars. Actually, they will be more like tiny airplanes or helicopters. Able to drive on highways and then quickly lift off, they will be able to hover high above the ground and then park in your driveway. Nearly a dozen companies have already developed early versions of the flying car. Another technology already used in some high-speed trains, magnetic levitation, may allow cars to "float" a few feet above the road without wheels.

Space flight for tourists. NASA and the U.S. Air Force have handled almost all manned U.S. space flights for the past half century. But in the last few years, a few companies have developed rockets that will take a small group of people into space for the ride of their lives. Regular flights are not expected to start for several more years, but a few of these companies are already taking reservations.

Computers in your skin. Today, people carry around wallets that contain their money, library card, driver's license, medical insurance card, and a bunch of other items. By putting a single chip underneath the skin on your arm (where you can't feel or see it), the need for a wallet and ID will be eliminated. You can store all your information in the chip and then wave your arm in front of a cash register or a library scanner and the information will be transferred to other computers. Several hundred people in the world already have embedded chips that are used for medical emergencies (a doctor can scan them to get a patient's medical history immediately). Eventually, it will be used to help track movements of convicted criminals or used to make sure children don't get lost. The chip won't quite make you a robot, but it will be the first step in combining computers with humans.

The end of coins and cash. Electronic wallets that act just like cash have already been tested in Europe and parts of the U.S. Much like subway or bus cards, they are loaded up with money from a bank or specialized machine that is deducted when purchases are made. So start collecting your coins now, because someday they'll just be a distant memory. But, hey! What happens if you need to flip heads or tails for something? Maybe scientists better figure that out, too.

Microscopic machines. A nanometer is a billionth of a meter. That's incredibly small, especially when you consider that one strand of your hair is 80,000 nanometers wide. Nanotechnology is the science of creating materials and devices measured in nanometers, meaning their size is down there at the level of atoms and molecules.

Using components no larger than a few molecules, scientists will build machines so small you can't even see hem. For example, these tiny machines might be injected into humans to clear away blood clots or cancerous cells. Manufacturers are already using nanotechnology to develop materials that are stronger, yet lighter, than steel. Some scientists worry about nanomachines getting into the air and people breathing them in, but we're not going to be at that level for a long time. But it still makes for an interesting idea: Can you picture someone sneezing a mini factory out of their nose?

One thing you probably won't see: teleportation. That's the transmitting of objects and people from one place to another by disintegrating them on one end, sending their particles (or digital versions) to another place, and reintegrating them on that end. It's a great science-fiction idea, but it isn't going to happen anytime soon. It's been estimated that it would take more computing power than has ever existed just to figure out how to encode the atoms of one single person before disintegrating them. That doesn't count figuring out how to put them back together again, which we think is the most important part. Especially for the person being disintegrated.

GREAT MYSTERIES: FAKE

CROP CIRCLES ARE strange patterns visible above large fields. They have appeared for centuries. Some are caused by fields that have been planted over ancient stone buildings or fortresses. Irrigation patterns cause others. In the 1970s, very intricate patterns began appearing in England—with no explanation. Some people believed that either aliens were creating the designs with their spacecraft, or that bizarre wind patterns were cutting through the fields. Finally, several pranksters admitted to creating the patterns by tying planks to the back of their trucks and dragging them through the fields.

IN 1912, workmen in a quarry in Piltdown, England found skull fragments. The pieces were brought to the British Museum, which made a stunning announcement. The skull belonged to a long-sought-after "missing link," the ancient being that marked the evolutionary transition from apes to humans. For 40 years, the skull of Piltdown Man was considered one of the most important fossils on Earth. Then in 1953, the British Museum determined through microscopic analysis that the Piltdown skull had been made from a human head and an orangutan's jaw, and treated with special chemicals to make it appear old. To this day, no one has identified the perpetrator of this elaborate hoax that fooled scientists for half a century.

WHILE DIGGING A well in Cardiff, New York, during the autumn of 1869, workers came upon the petrified body of a 10-foot-tall giant. The discovery was widely reported, and the owner of the farm charged people to see it, believing it to be a huge, prehistoric man. The farmer eventually sold his Cardiff Giant to a nearby museum, where it became so popular that P.T. Barnum, the showman who founded what later became the Ringling Brothers and Barnum & Bailey Circus, made a copy of it to show in his own museum. A year later, however, the farmer and his cousin admitted that the giant was a hoax. They had created it out of stone simply to spite a neighbor who believed in giants.

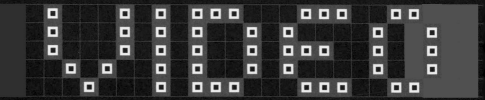

IN ORDER TO GET FAMILIAR WITH THE different kinds of video games, you have to know the lingo. Here are some acronyms from the online video game world.

RPG—Role-Playing Game
MMOG—Massively Multiplayer Online Game
MMORPG—Massively Multiplayer Online Role-Playing Game
BBMMORPG—Browser-Based Massive Multiplayer Online Role-Playing Game
MMOSG—Massively Multiplayer Online Social Game
MMORTS—Massively Multiplayer Online Real-Time Strategy

MMOFPS—Massively Multiplayer On First-Person Shooter
MMOTG—Massively Multiplayer On Tycoon Game

MOST POPULAR ONLINE GAMES THE WORLD

Video games are popular all over the wo They're certainly more fun than homew and louder, too. If you're playing them, you one of millions and millions of others who also battling it out online and on their com ers and TV screens. Most of them require you enter a strange universe where you g choose your avatar (the on-screen versio

as you prepare
attle evil and successfully complete lots of
sions.

World of Warcraft has more than eight mil-
subscribers, making it the biggest multi-
er online game in the world. RuneScape is
largest free online game with more than
million active players.

ld of Warcraft—WoW is a fantasy world
bited by everything from humans and
nes to ogres and the undead. You select
kind of "being" you want to represent you,
then head off across a planet where you
t monsters and seek fame and fortune.

Lineage 1 and 2—Originally developed in Korea, Lineage is hugely popular in Asia. The different versions of Lineage take you back to a medieval world filled with knights, wizards, and elves.

RuneScape—Gielinor is your home in RuneScape, where you attempt to live a life just like on Earth, running a business and working with other people. You also have to spend your days fighting beasts ranging from bears to dragons—which probably isn't like your life on Earth.

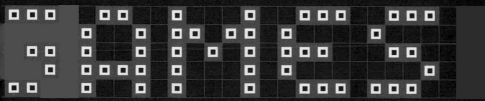

Final Fantasy XI—This game has become so popular that there are now movies, TV shows, and books based on it. When you enter Final Fantasy, be prepared to spend your time saving the world from evil villains and nasty corporations who want to control everything.

Everquest I and II—You seek out treasure and learn to build your own weapons in Everquest. With more than 4,000 zones of play, there are lots of monsters to face before you're finished—if you live that long.

***Star Wars* Galaxies**—Enter this game as a Wookiee, a human smuggler, or any number of other species from the popular *Star Wars* movies. As you fly through the universe, you're going to be spending a lot of time riding on landspeeders and meeting up with Ewoks.

City of Heroes/City of Villains—Deciding to become a superhero and choosing your costume is part of the CoH and CoV world, where you must stop criminals from ruining your day. The local newspaper alerts you to the loca-

tion of bank robberies and prison break and from there it's up to you to save the c

Eve—Cut off from the Earth after traveli a distant galaxy, you need to help colonize build new worlds. But there are lots of c species that don't want you to succeed, and ready to fight you the moment you show

MOST POPULAR KIDS' VIDEO GAME SERIES OF ALL TIME

There have been nearly 200 million S Mario Bros. games sold, with Pokemon ing in at close to 160 million. Odds are yo played one or more of them and have own favorite.

Super Mario Bros.—Mario is the most ognized video game character in the wor lot like Mickey Mouse is for ca oons. He called Jumpman when he orig lly appe in Donkey Kong, but was given the r Mario to honor Mario Segale, the man provided office space for Nintendo's Amer headquarters.

kemon—The name Pokemon is a short-
d combination of "pocket monsters." There
nearly 500 different Pokemon creatures.

al Fantasy—This video game was given
name because the man who designed it was
nning on retiring after he created it, mak-
it his "final" game. People clamored for
e after it was released, and there are now
past 12 Final Fantasy games.

Donkey Kong—Players will notice that
there is no donkey in Donkey Kong. The original name was Stubborn Gorilla, which
sounded kind of lame. The designers then
chose Kong to identify the gorilla character,
and the word "donkey" was added because the
ape was "stubborn like a donkey."

Sonic the Hedgehog—When Sega decided
to find a new mascot, they settled on a drawing for an animal who was code-named "Mr.
Needlemouse." This cartoon character would
eventually evolve into a hedgehog who turned
blue from the shock waves he encountered by
running at supersonic speed.

Gran Turismo—This game is named for
"grand tours," the long-distance auto
races that sometimes can last for several
days. We're especially fond of Gran Turis
mo and its high-speed racing and the
variety of courses. Sure beats sitting in a
real car stuck in a traffic jam.

DO NOT TRADE OR THROW OUT!

- 1999 First Edition Black Star Pikachu card—$30–$80

- Extremely Limited Edition Ultra-Rare Shrink SJC-EN003 (Yu-Gi-Oh)—$3,500
  (Reader, help us out here. We can't find the year for this card. When was it first issued?)

- 1997 First Edition of *Harry Potter and the Philosopher's Stone.* Published in England (the name was changed to *Sorcerer's Stone* in America), there were only about 500 of these hardcover first British editions of the book.—$20,000

- 1936 World Wide Howie Morenz #18 [Hockey card]—$50,000

- 1935 Bronko Nagurski #24 Chicle [Football card]—$240,000

- 1910 Honus Wagner T-206 Baseball Card—Over $2,000,000

BILLIONS

BILLIONAIRES HAVE A LOT OF MONEY. More money than you probably know. To show you just how big a billion is, let's make a billion dollars equal to a billion seconds. Guess how much a billion seconds is. Seems like it might be a year or two, right? Uh-uh. A billion seconds is almost 32 years. That translates to a lot of dollar bills.

How about a billion minutes? That equals 19 centuries, almost 2,000 years. A billion minutes from now it will be the year 3908.

WHO ARE THE WORLD'S RICHEST people, and how did they get that way? Basically, you have to be smart, focused, and being born rich doesn't hurt.

Bill Gates ($50 billion) created Microsoft, whose software, odds on, you've used. He started out as a teenager who spent every free moment learning early computers. His home is designed to modify the light, temperature, and sound in each room to the preferences each visitor has encoded on a microchip. The house and the land it stands on are valued at $113 million.

Warren Buffett ($42 billion) is a smart investor. His license plate reads THRIFTY, and he is, still living in the house he bought in 1958 for $31,500.

Gates and Buffett give away a good deal of their money, focusing in particular on improving education, just as Andrew Carnegie did. He made his pile as the toughest of the steel men in the 1800s, then paid for a good many of the public libraries around the country.

Carlos Slim Helu ($30 billion), the richest man in Latin America, lives in Mexico, and used inherited money to make smart investments in communications. His father was born in Lebanon and arrived in Mexico in 1902. Carlos made his fortune in the Internet age, but says he is more comfortable writing on paper than on a laptop.

Ingvar Kamprad ($28 billion) has been selling stuff ever since he was a teenager growing up in Sweden. He is responsible for Ikea stores—makers and sellers of inexpensive furniture someone you know has in their home. He lives modestly, owning a 1993 car and riding buses whenever possible. But he is not timid, saying, "Only those who are asleep make no mistakes."

Lakshmi Mittal ($23.5 billion) was born in India and now lives in England. He used money he inherited to create the world's largest steel company. His London home cost $127 million, just twice the $60 million he spent on his daughter's wedding.

Paul Allen ($22 billion) helped found Microsoft, and owns the Seattle Seahawks and SpaceShipOne—which is going to sell rides into space to the wealthy and curious. He has founded museums devoted to things he is interested in, such as music from Jimi Hendrix, World War II aircraft, and science fiction.

48 6F 77 20 6D 61 6E 79 20 6D 69 6C 65 73 20 63 6F 75 6C 64 20 61 20 4D 63 4C 61 72
65 6E 20 46 31 20 74 72 61 76 65 6C 20 69 6E 20 37 35 20 73 65 63 6F 6E 64 73 3F

GREAT MYSTERIES: SPOOKY

AREA 51

THERE IS A SECTION OF land near Groom Lake, Nevada, over which no planes are allowed to fly and which people without special clearance are forbidden to enter. It is owned by the U.S. government and is known as Area 51. The government tests secret weapons and technology here. And because it is off-limits to just about everyone, it is rumored that it also serves as a storage facility for things the government doesn't want anyone to see. This includes the remains of dead aliens whose bodies were allegedly recovered from a crash site in Roswell, New Mexico.

On July 1947, a rancher in Roswell found a strange object, composed of what looked like damaged aluminum foil and rubber, on his property. The U.S. Army claimed it was the remains of a weather balloon, but in the years since, the rancher's family and various military people involved in analyzing the material claimed that it wasn't a weather balloon at all: It was the remains of a crashed UFO and, even more important, that alien bodies were found at the ranch. There are those who think

that the real work going on at Area 51 is an attempt to rebuild the UFO from that crash.

MA: *There are those who think that monsters live under their beds, too. What about the idea that the Earth is flat? Some people still believe that; and there are a whole bunch of folks who claim we never went to the moon. Some people will believe anything.*

HPN: *The government has kept people away from Area 51 for decades. There are no public roads leading to it, and the base is surrounded by guard dogs, fences, and soldiers. Something's going on that regular people aren't supposed to see. . . .*

THE GHOST SHIP

ON DECEMBER 4, 1872, a sailing ship named the *Mary Celeste* was found floating off the coast of Portugal. When sailors from a passing ship boarded the *Mary Celeste,* they found no people on it. Everything was in place onboard, from the food to the cargo to the sailors' belongings. If it had been attacked by pirates, all those things would have been

taken. If there had been a violent storm, the boat would have suffered some damage. None of the sailors who sailed on the *Mary Celeste* were ever heard from, and no one knows where they went.

THE TUNGUSKA EVENT

IN A REMOTE AREA OF Russia known as Tunguska, on the morning of June 30, 1908, a tremendous explosion destroyed an entire forest, blasted buildings, and broke windows for hundreds of miles in every direction. Witnesses claimed to see a strange light in the sky as the blast occurred. Some said that it resembled a flying saucer. Scientists didn't investigate for more than a decade, due in part to how isolated Tunguska was and Russia's involvement in World War I. But when they did finally test for chemicals and elements in Tunguska's soil, they claimed that a comet or asteroid had probably exploded just before it hit the Earth. These objects should have left a crater in the ground, yet there was no crater from the blast—only miles of flattened trees and scorched earth. Could something stranger have blown p in that forest—something ike a UFO? We still don't now for sure....

MA: *Could it have been a UFO? Sure, except for the minor fact that there is not the slightest evidence that it was.*

PN: *Ah, but the beauty of it is that there's also no evidence that it wasn't a UFO. And even today, a century later, scientists can't say exactly what it was. We live in a universe with billions of galaxies and more planets than we can count. I'll bet there's probably some really interesting stuff out there, and it would be cool to think that maybe—just maybe— some of it has actually found its way here.*

BERMUDA TRIANGLE

THE BERMUDA TRIANgle is an area that is located between Florida, Puerto Rico, and Bermuda. Over the past century, more than 1,000 boats and planes have disappeared in this area, some for unknown reasons. As far back as 1492, Christopher Columbus reported strange lights in the area. From that point on, things got really weird. Five U.S. Navy aircraft disappeared there without a trace in 1945, followed by airliners, yachts, sailboats, and large ships.

The U.S. Coast Guard has published documents stating that it "does not recognize the existence of the so-called Bermuda Triangle as a geographic area of specific hazard to ships or planes. In a review of many aircraft and vessel losses in the area over the years, there has been nothing discovered that would indicate that casualties were the result of anything other than physical causes. No extraordinary factors have ever been identified." Whatever the explanation, vessels keep disappearing there. Some authors have proposed that the area, also called the Devil's Triangle, is home to a time warp that transports the missing craft to alternate universes or other dimensions.

AMELIA EARHART

A PIONEERING PILOT, Amelia Earhart was the first woman to fly solo across the Atlantic Ocean and the first to fly nonstop across the United States. She was one of the country's biggest celebrities when she announced plans in 1937 to fly all the way around the world accompanied by just one navigator, Fred Noonan. Media reports followed their progress all over the world.

The two were flying the last 7,000 miles of their flight from New Guinea to Howland Island (about 1,600 miles from Hawaii) when radio communications became garbled. Then contact was lost. Earhart and Noonan did not arrive at Howland Island, yet distress signals were picked up from their plane by radio operators around the Pacific Ocean for the next several days. Despite the most extensive search effort by the U.S. Navy and Coast Guard up to that time—nine ships and 66 planes at a cost of more than $4 million—neither Earhart, Noonan, nor their plane were ever found.

D.B. COOPER

ON THE NIGHT BEFORE Thanksgiving in 1971, one of the first hijackers of an American plane threatened to blow up an airliner over Washington State if he was not given $200,000. He was dressed in a business suit and his ticket identified him as Dan Cooper. The pilot agreed to his demands and landed the plane. Cooper allowed the other passengers to get off, and was given the money along with four parachutes. The pilot took off again, and sometime during the flight, Cooper jumped out the rear door with the money and a parachute. He has never been found, but in 1980, $5,800 of the ransom money was found in the Columbia River by a family on a picnic.

WORLD'S GRI

DAREDEVILS

NIAGARA FALLS TIGHTROPE WALKERS—THE GREAT FARINI AND BLONDIN

Although not the biggest falls in the world, Niagara is one of the widest falls, with more than six million cubic feet of water spilling over its 173-foot height every second. The Great Farini (William Hunt) and Charles Blondin were tightrope walkers in the 1850s who competed to see who could do the most outrageous stunt over Niagara Falls. Their wires were suspended 160 feet over the falls, and they performed feats that have never been attempted again. Both pushed wheelbarrows across the wire at this height; that was considered an easy stunt. Blondin carried one of his friends out on his back, and once carried a small stove and cooked himself a breakfast omelet on the wire. Farini washed his clothes

on the wire by pulling water up from the f in a bucket, and even lowered himself dow a passing ship, then climbed back up agai

THE SOLO SAILOR—SIR FRANCIS CHICESTER

This 65-year-old British sailor went all way around the world in his boat in just n months and one day. He lived on his 54-sailing yacht all alone during 1966 and 19 stopped only once (in Sydney, Australia), logged a total of 28,500 miles, going from to west against the prevailing winds.

THE MAN WHO WALKED BETWEEN THE TOWERS—PHILIPPE PETIT

Using an arrow, aerialist Philippe Petit sh wire between the twin towers of the W Trade Center using an arrow on the morn

TEST

...ugust 14, 1974. He then walked out on the
..., more than 1,000 feet above New York
... He crossed the distance between the
...dings eight times, even pausing to lie down
...he wire.

...YSCRAPING—ALAIN ROBERT

...a dreary Christmas Day in 2004,
...in Robert climbed up the outside of
...t was then the tallest building in
... world, the Taipei 101 in Taiwan.
... building is 1,679 feet high, and
...ert climbed up the windows all the
... to the top in pouring rain, using
...his hands and a rope. He has
...bed skyscrapers all over the
...ld with nothing more than
...bare hands.

SPEED RECORDS

SPEED RECORDS ARE OFTEN MEASURED against the speed of sound, which is approximately 761.18 miles per hour at ground level. This is known as Mach 1, named after the man who discovered it, Ernst Mach.

Many car and motorcycle speed records have been set at the Bonneville Salt Flats, a dry, salt lake in Utah. The salt prevents plants from growing and occasional rains pound the salt flat—so there are no bumps or natural obstacles. This makes it the best flat surface (and the biggest, at 150 square miles) in the world for testing really fast vehicles.

Vehicles of all sorts have allowed humans to travel at speeds of hundreds of miles per hour on Earth. In comparison, the fastest sprinter can only reach a speed of about 23 mph.

Chuck Yeager was the first human to fly faster than the speed of sound. On October 14, 1947, he flew an experimental plane called the *X-1* to Mach 1.06—roughly 660 mph. The *X-1* was built like a missile with a cockpit—not a standard airplane—and it shook almost to the point of disintegrating before he slowed it down. Up until Yeager accomplished this feat, many scientists thought that the shock waves from a sonic boom would destroy an airplane.

FASTEST BOAT
Ken Warby piloted his jet boat at a speed of 317 mph on the Blowering Dam in New South Wales, Australia, on October 8, 1978.

FASTEST MOTORCYCLE
Chris Carr took his motorcycle up to 354 mph in Utah on September 5, 2006.

FASTEST AUTOMOBILE
Andy Green drove the custom Thrust Super-SonicCar to 763 mph (Mach 1.02) in Nevada on October 15, 1997.

FASTEST PLANE
Air Force Major William J. Knight flew his *X-15* at 4,520 mph (Mach 6.7) at an altitude of almost 20 miles above the United States on October 3, 1967.

Ekat a kced fo sdrac, gnidulcni owt srekoj. Edivid eht sdrac pu gnoma flesruoy dna owt sdneirf. Woh ynam sdrac seod hcae fo uoy evah?

SPEEDS...
IN MILES PER HOUR

0.03	A fast snail (33 hours to go a mile)
3–5	Walking
15	Average bicycling speed
25	Top speed of a running human
30	Top speed of a running dog
60	Typical highway speed for cars
65–70	Top speed of both a cheetah and a sailfish
70	Fast football pass
103	Top speed of a pitcher's fastball
130	Fast tennis serve
180	High-speed train
200	Diving speed of the world's fastest bird, the peregrine falcon
260	Top speed of the fastest sports car, Volkswagen's Bugatti Veyron
300	Wind speed of the strongest tornadoes
625	Cruising jet airliner
761	Sound
763	Current land speed record (fastest anyone has ever driven a vehicle on land)
1,038	Earth rotating
1,300	Cruising jet fighter
1,800	Bullet from high-powered rifle
17,500	Space shuttle in orbit
25,000	Velocity required for a rocket to break Earth's gravity
670,616,629	Light

DATES

TRANSPORTA

1807 — Robert Fulton, having experimented with building a submarine, shifts his interests and launches the *Claremont*, the first successful commercial steamboat in America.

1825 — Erie Canal opens, linking New York Harbor with the Midwest and spurring a flurry of canal building across the country. But even as canals are being built, a new form of transportation is about to make them obsolete (see 1828).

1828 — The Baltimore and Ohio Railroad, the first westbound train tracks in America, begins construction.

1860 — Pony Express begins in April, with riders said to be as young as 11, but it only lasts until October of the following year. Given how often it comes up in novels, you'd think ponies were expressing all over the West, but no way.

1869 — Golden Spike ceremony on May 10, at Promontory Summit, Utah, celebrating completion of the first transcontinental railroad.

1893 — After seeing a gasoline engine at the 1886 Ohio State Fair, Charles Duryea and his brother Frank design and begin building an automobile. Seven years later in Springfield, Massachusetts, they complete the first successful run of an automobile in the U.S.

1908 — First paved road built in America, near Detroit.

1927 — Ford stops making Model T cars, having sold 15 million since 1908, half of all the new cars in America.

G9

44 6C 63 6B 7A 67 63 70 20 6B 79 76 20 72 65 6A 6E 76 69 6A 20 6B 66 20 58 2I
6B 6E 76 63 6D 76 20 72 65 75 20 58 2D 6B 6E 66 20 6B 66 20 78 76 6B 20 6B 7
76 20 72 65 6A 6E 76 69 20 6B 66 20 6B 79 7A 6A 20 68 6C 76 6A 6B 7A 66 65 2

) KNOW

IN AMERICA

irst U.S. commercial airline flight, from St. Petersburg to Tampa, lorida.	**1914**
iomeone invents the skateboard.	**1950**
ngineer Wendell Moore invents the "Small Rocket Lift Device," a rocket elt for one person.	**1953**
ederal Aid Highways Act provides funds to create highways linking the ation.	**1956**
ord creates a big marketing campaign for its new car, the Edsel. But it is gly, expensive for the time, and no one likes it very much. The company oses what would be $2.25 billion today.	**1958**
arold Graham flies for 13 seconds in a rocket belt, or jet pack. Despite ne obvious appeal of this way of getting around, neither the govern- nent, the army, nor private individuals rush to use the belt.	**1961**
londa sells the Insight, the first mass-produced (widely available) car in america that runs on a combination of electricity and gasoline. Oh well, uess we'll have to be content with cars that do less harm to the envi- onment, instead of dashing around on ponies, or flying in cool jet packs.	**1999**
enis Tito pays somewhere from $12 million to $20 million (no one is elling) to spend seven days on a Russian-made Soyuz spaceship, ecoming the first American space tourist.	**2001**

Did you konw ppeloe can read wrdos wsohe ltretes are smbcalerd as lnog as the fsirt and lsat ltreets saty at the bieningng and end? Prtety animazg! Aaywny, here is a hint for Giadarun pzzlue G6: Write eervy wrod baakdrcws.

HOW DOES IT WORK?

MP3
Player
& iPod

MUSIC HAS BEEN RECORDED and played on many different types of machines since the late 1800s. These machines all have one thing in common: They change the sound of music (air vibrations, actually) into electrical signals and then "burn" those signals onto a material or device. To create vinyl records, electrical signals were used to vibrate a needle that cut grooves into plastic. On tape recorders, magnets format tiny particles of iron on tape to match the incoming signals. CDs use lasers to burn the same types of signals into microscopic bumps and divots on plastic disks.

MP3s are the newest format for storing and playing music, designed for use on computers and high-tech machines like iPods. MP3 is a computer file that uses a mathematical representation of songs that have usually been recorded in a music studio. As the MP3 file is being created, it eliminates some of the sounds from the original recording that can't be heard by humans. When this is done, the file ends up being a small digital file that isn't much different than a word-processing document. These small files are then stored on a hard disk or a computer chip.

The iPod has become the most popular MP3 player because of its cool styling and how easy it is to use. It acts as both the storage device and the player; you don't have the music contained on one thing and then played on another (like individual CDs that have to be put into CD players).

By the way, MP3 stands for Motion Picture Experts Group, Audio Layer 3, which is a long name for the organization that decides how computers will read videos and songs. The name MP3 is really all you need to know.

Here's an interesting comparison of how far our music technology has come.

One vinyl album = 45 minutes of music (two sides) 3 oz

One cassette tape = 90 minutes of music (two sides) 1.4 oz

One CD = 80 minutes of music (one side) .6 oz

One MP3 player = 1,000 hours of music (no sides) 4.8 oz

Thneqvna chmmyr T14 vf rapelcgrq jvgu n fhofgvghgvba pvcure. Gur xrl vf ARJWBOSVKZETYHPXFUNMLGICQD.

MONSTER

ALMOST EVERY CULTURE IN THE WORLD has stories about monstrous beasts that ro
about hidden in forests or in lakes or high up in the mountains. Scientists have tried to pr
their existence for years, but these "monster hunters" have never found enough evidence
say for certain whether they are real.

Should you decide to go monster hunting on your own, you could look for the beasts
this list—if you think they might actually exist.

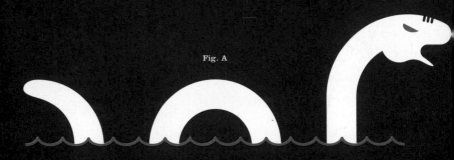

Fig. A

CHAMP (Fig. A)

Champ is a sea monster alleged to reside in
Lake Champlain, which is located on the
Vermont–New York border. Local residents
claim it has a long, snakelike body and a huge
head. You'll need to do some scuba diving or
have a small submarine to search down in the
400-foot depths of the cold lake. Either that,
or wait for a very long time on the shore of
Lake Champlain. If you do find it, don't harm
it in any way. Both New York and Vermont
have passed laws protecting Champ—if anyone actually ever finds it.

MA: *Funny thing about these lake monster*
they are so easy to spot, except when any
is looking.

HPN: *Have you ever tried to locate a*
when someone suddenly shouts, "Look o
there!" Water creatures almost never s
their heads or bodies out into the air wh
they can be seen. If they did, you'd be see
dozens of sharks and whales and squ
every time you went swimming in the oce

A5   Irst-fay eneral-gay int-hay: E-thay answers-way o-tay e-thay Uardian-gay uzzles-pay are-way
umbers-nay at-thay ou-yay ill-way eed-nay o-tay ow-knay or-fay e-thay Aster-may uzzles-pay.

HUNTING

CHUPACABRA (Fig. B)

...u are going to want to be especially careful ...hunting for this doglike beast. It is said to ...nd on two legs and have a wicked temper. ...art your search on grazing lands in remote ...rts of Latin America and the United States, ...ere the chupacabra likes to eat the local ...tle, especially goats (the name means "goat ...cker" in Spanish). It would help to bring a ...geatcher; some scientists believe that it ...y actually be a type of canine mutation. ...1 will have to be careful and quick: The ...upacabra is said to be able to eat any kind ...animal in just a few minutes.

BIGFOOT (SASQUATCH) (Fig. C)

Described as a huge, manlike creature standing about 7 feet tall and covered completely in hair, he roams the forests of North America. Stories of him have been around for more than a century. Try to track him by his footprints after it rains. Bring a video camera, too. There is one very fuzzy video of a creature that the cameraman claims was Bigfoot. Watch out for fakes: The son of one man admitted that his father walked around in fake feet to trick people into thinking Bigfoot was around.

Fig. B

Fig. C

Fig. E

Fig. D

YETI (THE ABOMINABLE SNOWMAN) (Fig. E)

This one is going to be pretty hard to tra[ck] down since it lives up in the Himalaya[n] Mountains. That means you're going to ha[ve] to do some climbing up through ice peaks [to] find him. Similar to Bigfoot, the yeti is said [to] be a very tall, manlike beast that seeks refu[ge] in ice caves. Since he lives up among the hig[h]est mountains in the world, you will ne[ed] backpacking equipment, oxygen tanks for t[he] high altitude, and a local guide called [a] sherpa to lead you on your search. Look [for] his footprints, which many climbers ha[ve] seen in the deep snow.

MA: *So, you have climbers who are dizzy fr[om] lack of oxygen seeing fuzzy footprints—I w[on]der why that seems unconvincing?*

HPN: *Yeah, they're seeing fuzzy footprint[s] several miles up a mountain where no a[ni]mal is known to exist. Something is mak[ing] those footprints and, dizzy or not, lots [of] climbers have seen a dark figure walk[ing] around on two legs.*

LOCH NESS MONSTER (Fig. D)

Known as "Nessie," this sea serpent lives in a deep Scottish lake (*loch* is Scottish for "lake"). You're going to need scuba equipment or a lot of patience. While Nessie has been photographed by several people who were allegedly in the right place at the right time, researchers in submarines have been unable to find it. The lake is incredibly cold and dark—you'll need a wet suit and some underwater lights—and a popular theory is that the monster is a form of dinosaur called a plesiosaur that may have been trapped under ice when other dinosaurs became extinct.

Fig. F

~RSEY DEVIL (Fig. F)

~is may be the scariest monster to look for.
~'re going to have to go deep into New Jer-
~'s Pine Barrens, a bleak and uninhabited
~etch of dark forest in the south part of the
~te. This is the supposed home of a large,
~nged creature with glowing eyes and hooves.
~s best to look for the Jersey Devil after a
~wfall, and check out rooftops for its hoof-
~nts after the beast has swooped down for a
~t. Make sure to look around nearby farms,
~he monster has often been accused of eat-
~ chickens. And listen carefully; it appar-
~ly emits a horrendous scream.

MA: *I know the Jersey Devils are real—in fact, I root for them. They're my local hockey team.*

HPN: *Laugh it up, but your favorite team takes its name from the mysterious New Jersey monster, which was first described in the late 1700s—more than a hundred years before the National Hockey League was even formed!*

Reader, send us your evidence of these or other monsters.

THINGS TO REMEMBER

YOUR WHOLE LIFE

THERE ARE SOME FACTS you'll need to have at your fingertips for your whole life. We've put together some ways to make them easier to remember. Someday, you'll thank us for this. If you don't forget.

☑ When turning almost anything, from screwdrivers to the caps on soda bottles, "right is tight and left is loose." Right will turn things off or tighten them; left will turn them on or unscrew them.

☑ When spelling words, it's "I before E, except after C." Check it out: believe vs. receive, relief vs. receipt, thief vs. deceive.

☑ The names of planets in order from the sun: My Very Educated Mother Just Served Us Nachos (Pluto was dropped, remember?). This is the way to remember Mercury, Venus, Earth, Mars, Jupiter, Saturn, Uranus, and Neptune.

☑ Number of days in a month:
"30 days hath September,
April, June, and November."
All the rest have 31 (except for February, which has 28…and sometimes 29!).

☑ The names of the Great Lakes: HOMES (Huron, Ontario, Michigan, Erie, Superior).

☑ Left vs. Right: If you are getting left and right confused, hold up your thumbs and first fingers in the shape of an "L." The correct facing "L" will be your left hand.

☑ Here's how to remember the spelling of "separate": Separate is A RAT of a word to spell.

U.S. STATES AND CAPITALS

WE CANNOT THINK OF ANYTHING more mind-numbingly boring than a list of states and their capitals. But it does come in handy in games, and there is some fun to be had if you go just a bit outside of the ordinary.

STATE (year of statehood)	CAPITAL	REALLY?
Alabama (1819)	Montgomery	Now, this is confusing. Montgomery is in Montgomery County, but the county is named after Lemuel Montgomery, who died in the War of 1812, and the city is named after Richard Montgomery, who died fighting in the American Revolution. Good thing the state isn't named Montgomery.
Alaska (1959)	Juneau	Juneau has no roads linking it to the rest of the state.
Arizona (1912)	Phoenix	The canals that bring water to Phoenix are built on top of ancient Indian waterways. Like the mythical phoenix, the new rises out of the old.
Arkansas (1836)	Little Rock	Guess what, the capital is named after ... a little rock in the Arkansas River that people used as a marker.
California (1850)	Sacramento	Sacramento is located near where John Sutter owned a huge tract of land. The gold that set off the 1849 gold rush was found on Sutter's land, and he eventually lost it all.
Colorado (1876)	Denver	Denver is the only city to win a bid to host an Olympics (1976 Winter Games) and then turn it down.
Connecticut (1788)	Hartford	In 1814, delegates from throughout New England met in Hartford, threatening to secede from the U.S., which they thought was mishandling the War of 1812.

Delaware (1787)	Dover	Dover is the only capital to have a volunteer fire department, and it is one of just five capitals that is not on an interstate highway.
Florida (1845)	Tallahassee	Floridians picked Tallahassee as their capital in 1824 because it was midway between the two most important cities of the time, St. Augustine and Pensacola.
Georgia (1788)	Atlanta	Atlanta is the proud home of a 38-foot-tall Coca-Cola bottle made out of baseball equipment (not to mention Georgia's largest city).
Hawaii (1959)	Honolulu	In the native language of Hawaii, Honolulu means "place of shelter," and from 1809 on, the royal family of Hawaii lived there.
Idaho (1890)	Boise	Originally a fort, Boise was built where a stretch of the Oregon Trail crossed the routes to nearby mines.
Illinois (1818)	Springfield	You've got to visit the Pearson Museum in Springfield. Who could pass up exhibits on leeches and the great advantages of letting them suck your blood?
Indiana (1816)	Indianapolis	Indianapolis was an idea before it was a city—when Indiana became a state, they decided to build a capital as close to its center as possible. So, first they picked the site, then built Indianapolis.
Iowa (1846)	Des Moines	In 1843, Captain James Allen suggested building a fort where the Des Moines and Raccoon Rivers crossed—only he wanted to call it Fort Raccoon. Too bad the War Department insisted on calling it Fort Des Moines. It would have been nice to have an animal state capital.
Kansas (1861)	Topeka	Topeka means "a good place to dig prairie potatoes," but don't have visions of french fries. "Prairie potatoes" are herbs.

Kentucky (1792)	Frankfort	Daniel Boone is buried in Frankfort, but also in Defiance, Missouri—no one is sure which grave has his real bones.
Louisiana (1812)	Baton Rouge	People have lived near Baton Rouge for more than 10,000 years. Early French settlers saw a large red tree that marked the boundary between two native groups. The French called the tree a "baton rouge," a red stick.
Maine (1820)	Augusta	Augusta is home to Fort Western. Built in 1754, it is the oldest wooden fort in America.
Maryland (1788)	Annapolis	Annapolis was the nation's first peacetime capital, until the Founders went off to Philadelphia to draft the Constitution.
Massachusetts (1788)	Boston	Is there any possible reason why you won't be able to remember this?
Michigan (1837)	Lansing	Lansing was originally a scam—con artists sold land in a town that did not exist and was usually underwater.
Minnesota (1858)	Saint Paul	Looking for the world's largest snowman built out of plaster? You've found him; the 54-foot guy is in Saint Paul.
Mississippi (1817)	Jackson	Jackson is one of four state capitals named after presidents. See if you can find the other three.
Missouri (1821)	Jefferson City	If you have not found the next capital named after a president, you are fast asleep.
Montana (1889)	Helena	Helena was a gold rush town that yielded over three billion dollars worth of gold. Lucky miners built large mansions, which still stand.
Nebraska (1867)	Lincoln	The 911 emergency call system was invented in Lincoln—notice anything else about the name?
Nevada (1864)	Carson City	Named after the scout "Kit" Carson, Nevada's capital grew rapidly when the Comstock Lode of silver was discovered nearby.

New Hampshire (1788)	Concord	The statehouse in Concord was built in 1819 and is still used by the legislature, making it the oldest statehouse still used for its original purpose.
New Jersey (1787)	Trenton	George Washington's surprise attack on the British on December 26, 1776, took place in Trenton.
New Mexico (1912)	Santa Fe	Located 7,000 feet above sea level, Santa Fe is the highest state capital.
New York (1788)	Albany	If you go to Albany, keep your eyes peeled for the giant statue of a dog seated on top of a warehouse.
North Carolina (1789)	Raleigh	Raleigh was named after Sir Walter Raleigh, sponsor of the colony at Roanoke, which he never visited (*see* page 38).
North Dakota (1889)	Bismarck	Bismarck's name honors the "Iron Chancellor" who united Germany. Businessmen hoped to attract German immigrants.
Ohio (1803)	Columbus	Half of the people in America live within 500 miles of Columbus.
Oklahoma (1907)	Oklahoma City	Oklahoma City is the only capital that has a working oil well on the grounds of its capitol building.
Oregon (1859)	Salem	Salem is home to the world's smallest park—Waldo Park consists of just one Sierra Redwood planted in 1872.
Pennsylvania (1787)	Harrisburg	Though Native Americans lived in this area for thousands of years, the town of Harrisburg owes its origin to James Harris, who first set up a trading post on the site in 1710. Here's one case where the name of a city tells you its history.
Rhode Island (1790)	Providence	Providence's 58-foot statue of "Nibbles" the termite is said to be the largest insect replica in the world.

South Carolina (1788)	Columbia	The name Columbia was chosen over Washington in a 1786 vote, which is why there is still one more president's name capital to go.
South Dakota (1889)	Pierre	Named after a fort that was on the same site, Pierre is pronounced "peer"—here, but nowhere else.
Tennessee (1796)	Nashville	Nashville became the home of country music because a local insurance company decided to sponsor a radio station. In 1924, WSM ("we shield millions") came on the air and began broadcasting what became the Grand Ole Opry.
Texas (1845)	Austin	When Pappy Lee O'Daniel took office for his second term as governor of Texas in 1941, he held a barbecue here for 20,000 people, who ate 19,000 pounds of meat, helped down by 32,000 cups of coffee.
Utah (1896)	Salt Lake City	We know exactly when this city was created—it was established by Brigham Young and a small group of fellow Mormons on July 24, 1847, as Great Salt Lake City.
Vermont (1791)	Montpelier	With just 8,000 residents, Montpelier is the least-populous state capital.
Virginia (1788)	Richmond	Richmond became Virginia's capital in 1780, and just a year later Benedict Arnold, fighting for the British, burned it down. But the city survived, and he lost.
Washington (1889)	Olympia	The Native Americans who lived where Olympia is now called it the "Black Bear Place."
West Virginia (1863)	Charleston	The first street in the world to be paved entirely with bricks was created in Charleston in 1870.
Wisconsin (1848)	Madison	Home to one campus of the University of Wisconsin. Wonder where the name came from?
Wyoming (1890)	Cheyenne	Cheyenne Frontier Days is held here at the end over every July and said to be the largest rodeo in the world.

PEOPLE, PEOPLE EVERYWHERE . . .

THERE ARE AN ESTIMATED 6.6 BILLION people living right now on this planet. They reside in 193 different countries and dozens of territories and colonies, but more than half of all people live in just the five places listed below. Here's an interesting fact: One out of every three people in the world lives in China or India.

China	1.3 billion
India	1.1 billion
European Union	490 million
United States	300 million
Indonesia	250 million

The places with the most people are not always the biggest countries, in terms of land size. Check this out (square kilometers):

Russia	17,075,200
Antarctica	14,000,000
Canada	9,984,670
United States	9,826,630
China	9,596,960

While Russia fills some 17 million square kilometers, and Canada 9.9, nobody lives in most of that territory. Compare that to Monaco, an island country off the south of France, which has more than 32,000 people jammed into less than one square mile (which adds up to a density of 42,000 people per square mile). On the other hand, Mongolia has 2.8 million people spread out over nearly 605,000 square miles (with a population density of only five people per square mile).

With the exception of some deserts, badlands, and glaciers here and there, America's 9.6 million square kilometers are full of people. And fast-food places.

BASEBALL'S BEST

SIX MEN IN BASEBALL HISTORY HAVE HIT 300 home runs and stolen 300 bases. If you have trouble remembering those six names, it is much easier for the 500-500 club. It has exactly one member: Barry Bonds.

The first to make it to 300-300 was Willie Mays, then Andre Dawson, Bobby Bonds, and then Bobby's son Barry, who is also Willie's godson. More recent additions to the club are Steve Finley and Reggie Sanders.

PLAYER	SEASONS	HOME RUNS	BASES STOLEN
Willie Mays	1951–1945; 1954–1973	660	338 (led the National League in stolen bases four years in a row)
Bobby Bonds	1968–1981	332	461
Andre Dawson	1976–1996	438 (won the 1987 Home Run Derby)	314
Barry Bonds	1986–2007	762	514
Steve Finley	1989–2007	304	320
Reggie Sanders	1991–2007	305	304

ALL-AMERICAN

★ ★ ★ ★ ★ ★ ★ ★ ★

MICKEY D'S: With its nearly 13,000 McDonald's franchises, America has three times as many as Japan, at number two; and 13 times as many as Canada, number three.

WEALTH: America's total national income is twice that of Japan, in second; four times Germany, in third; and six times that of England, in fourth; France, just behind, is in fifth.

INTERNET USE: When we are not out eating or making money, we're on the Internet. America ranks first in Internet users, ahead of China, Japan, and India. Then comes Germany.

MT. EVEREST CLIMBING: Not all Americans, though, are burger-filled Net-surfers. Americans rank second in climbing Mt. Everest, with 178 climbers, ahead of Japan's 85, Russia's 67, and England's 60. The country that really excels at climbing Mount Everest is Nepal—which makes sense since the mountain straddles Nepal and Tibet, and people who live near it are skilled climbers. Some 532 Nepalese have scaled the world's highest mountain.

OLYMPIC MEDALS: America ranks first in all-time summer Olympic medals—and it isn't close. America's 2,116 is three and a half times second-place England's 638, and it is downhill from there to France's 598, Italy's 479, and Sweden's 469.

SOCCER: But, sad to say, there is one area where America is, let's face it, terrible. Brazil has won the most World Cup matches in soccer, with 64; Germany is second at 56; Italy third at 45; Argentina is fourth at 33. Though America tries, we are tied with Croatia for 24th. We've taken a big six matches.

BIGGER FISH EAT smaller fish, we all know that. But where does that chain begin? With the top predator, the animal so powerful and well-suited to where it lives that no other species treats it as a snack—no other species, that is, but humans. Here are some of the best of the best of predators:

American alligators eat whatever comes their way, from fish to spiders to raccoons, deer, or even bears and boys. The alligator gulps down its victim whole, then slowly digests it. Alligators live in wetlands throughout the southeastern United States. Though alligator attacks on humans are rare, this is one animal that will eat you if you wade into its path.

Bald eagles live throughout North America and typically eat fish, birds, and small rodents such as mice. They can lift about four pounds and fly off, so if they spot a vulnerable larger animal, such as a chicken, they will grasp it in their talons and try to carry it off.

Brown bears eat everything, from up to 40,000 moths in a day—which they catch by turning over rocks and exposing moths that cannot yet fly—to mushrooms, fish, squirrels, or a dead moose. They will attack people, but generally do not eat them. Brown bears live in mountainous regions in North America, Asia, and Europe.

Electric eels are not actually eels, they are knifefish. Adult eels eat other kinds of fish, which they shock in order to eat whole while the other fish is stunned but still alive. The current they create is as strong as a stun gun and keeps enemies away. It should also keep you away, because if a knifefish zaps you, it really hurts. Electric eels live in freshwater rivers in South America.

Great horned owls eat other birds, mammals such as rabbits, mice, or cats, and dine on fish or reptiles throughout North America and parts of South America. They sit on branches and watch for prey, then swoop down and grab what they want with their strong, sharp talons. Because of this ferocious attack, as well as the bands on their chests, the great horned owl is known as the "winged tiger."

Jaguars kill their prey in a special way; they use their powerful jaws to bite through the animal's skull into the brain. These large cats go after big animals such as deer and anacondas, but will even eat frogs, monkeys, or turtles. Jaguars live in Mexico and parts of Central and South America.

Killer whales (orcas) live in all of the world's oceans. Hunting in packs, called pods, the whales follow different strategies depending on what kind of food is most plentiful near where they live. Some prefer to follow schools of fish such as herring; others concentrate on mammals such as seals. Killer whales have even been known to attack great white sharks.

King cobras mainly eat other snakes, which is good because their venom is deadly, and for short periods

PREDATORS–
KINGS OF THE HILL

they can raise their heads up to human height. They live in South Asia.

Komodo dragons live on islands in Indonesia, where they eat everything from insects and birds to the bodies of horses and water buffalo. Their teeth have jagged edges for ripping flesh, and their mouths are filled with deadly bacteria (which does not harm them), so that an injured animal will soon die from infection, even if it survives an attack. While the dragons are usually about 8 feet long, some reach 10 feet.

Lions hunt in packs called prides, which usually include about two males and seven females. Lionesses do almost all of the actual hunting, but then males grab the kill and feed themselves first. Lions can hunt anything from rhinos and young elephants to giraffes and gnus, but they also take over kills made by other animals.

Polar bears eat whatever meat they can get, from seals, crabs, and walrus to birds, musk oxen, and reindeer. Their habitat in the Arctic Ocean area is in danger as global warming melts ice and raises water temperatures.

Snapping turtles will eat whatever they can get into their mouths, from insects to mammals to your fingers or toes. They live in North America.

Tigers are the world's largest cats. They are good swimmers and, whether on land or in the water, will take on crocodiles and snakes, as well as easier prey such as deer, pigs, and water buffalo. Today, most tigers live in South and East Asia.

KINGS OF ANCIENT HILLS

THESE GUYS ARE NO LONGER AROUND, and it is a good thing, too. They sound like the kind of monsters you read about in myths and legends, but they were real.

ALLOSAURUS. The name means "strange" lizard, because when scientists first found its bones, they looked different from other dinosaurs known at the time. One hundred and fifty million years ago, this guy was the dinosaur to beat in what later became North America. The biggest were some 35 feet long and they probably hunted in packs, had really sharp teeth, and were smart and strong.

ANDREWSARCHUS MONGOLIENSIS. "ANDREWS'S BEAST"—so named because Roy Chapman Andrews found its remains in Mongolia. At 13–18 feet long, these giant wolf-like animals lived 60 million years ago. They were so big and strong, they may have eaten beached whales, turtles, nearby mammals, and anything large and slow that crossed their path.

HOW TO

FIGHT OFF AN ALLIGATOR

DURING ONE WEEK IN 2006, three people in Florida were eaten by alligators. In the previous 50 years, only 17 people had been eaten. So, either the alligators got really hungry all of a sudden, or these three unlucky humans didn't know how to handle an angry gator.

Well, here's what you need to know in order not to become an alligator appetizer: An alligator has the strongest jaws of any creature; it can clamp down with a force of 2,000 pounds (Fig. A), which is enough to flip a car into the air. But—and this is a big but—alligators have almost zero force to open their jaws (Fig. B). The muscles that open their mouths are so weak that the jaws can be held shut with a rubber band. Or, in your case, with two hands.

If you've got an alligator on your tail, the best thing to do is run away from it in a zigzagging motion. But if it's so close that you can smell its breath (which typically smells like rotting, dead animals), then your best bet is to jump on its neck and clamp its mouth shut with your hands. And hold on tight. You'll feel like you're on a bucking bronco, but as long as the alligator can't open its mouth, you won't end up inside it. If you think you can do it with one hand, use the other to poke its eyes—hard.

By the way, alligators are found only in the United States and China. The rest of the world has crocodiles. And using your hands on crocodile jaws works just as well.

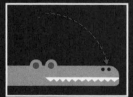

Fig. A - Strong

Fig. B - Weak

DISEASES YOU DEFINITELY DON'T WANT TO GET

ANTHRAX

This disease, which usually affects cattle, can be passed to people if they breathe in the spores from infected animals, or if the spores enter a cut on your skin. It infects your lungs and your intestines, breaking down the tissue and causing internal bleeding. Vomiting blood is one symptom, and inhaled anthrax almost always leads to certain death.

BOTULISM

A disease frequently transmitted in tainted food (especially in cans), it causes paralysis. First your facial muscles become paralyzed, and then the disease works its way down your body over the course of several days until just about everything is paralyzed and you can no longer breathe. The botulinum toxin may be the most poisonous substance known to man.

EBOLA

A viral disease that liquefies your internal organs and causes bleeding from every body opening. You get ebola by being exposed to the body fluids of an infected person, especially their saliva and blood. There is no cure once you get it.

PLAGUE

Plague is an actual disease caused by the Yersinia pestis bacteria, which is spread by rodents and fleas, and sometimes passes between people. It attacks your lungs and causes them to fill up with liquid. In some forms, it causes internal bleeding right under your skin, causing your flesh to turn a purplish black just before you die. During the 1300s, a plague known as the "Black Death" (from the grotesque discoloration of the victims' skin) killed 25 million people in Europe, one third of the population.

SMALLPOX

One of the most widespread diseases in history, it is easily passed from person to person by everything from touch to clothing. It attacks your entire body, causing infections and even brain inflammation. There have been numerous epidemics throughout history, and historians believe that smallpox probably killed off most of the Native American population after Europeans with the disease moved to the Americas. Another killed more than 100,000 people during the Revolutionary War. Thanks to vaccinations, smallpox has been successfully eliminated from most of the world. Samples of the deadly virus are stored in two vaults for future research: one in Atlanta, Georgia, and the other in Siberia.

THE BIGGEST MAN-MADE THIN

THERE'S SOMETHING incredibly cool about huge, enormous, and gigantic things, especially when they are man-made. Staring up at a skyscraper, standing up close to a huge jet—it makes you wonder just how big these things can really get. Guess what? We've got the answer below. And we are talking so gigantic and enormous, these things can only be called ginormous.

BUILDINGS

The world's tallest building is the Burj Dubai skyscraper in Dubai . . . and it isn't even finished yet. In July 2007, it became the tallest building in the world when construction reached 1,680 feet. But the builders are planning for a final height of over 2,500 feet, almost half a mile high. This would make it the tallest structure in history and twice as high as the Empire State Building. Previous "world's tallest" were Taiwan's Taipei 101, the Petronas Towers in Malaysia, the Sears Tower in Chicago, and New York's World Trade Center and Empire State Building.

The world's biggest building in terms of how much ground space it takes up is the Aalsmeer Flower Auction in the Netherlands. It covers almost 11 million square feet of space (most homes in the United States are only between one thousand and four thousand square feet). Close to 20 million flowers are sold in this building every day.

TUNNELS

The longest tunnels in the world are railroad tunnels that go underwater. Japan's Seikan Tunnel connects two islands and is the world's longest at 33.4 miles, of which 14.5 miles is under the seabed. The Channel Tunnel connecting England and France is the second-longest tunnel at 31 miles, but 24 of those miles are under the sea. The Channel Tunnel was dug at a depth of 150 feet under the floor of the English Channel.

The longest car tunnel is Norway's Laerdal Tunnel, which is 15.2 miles long and cuts through a mountain. Norwegian officials were s concerned about drivers get ting stressed driving throug a tunnel that long that the built four huge cave section that make drivers feel lik they're emerging into ope space.

TOWERS

The CN Tower in Toront Canada, is the world's talles structure, standing 1,81 feet tall. It was designed as TV and radio tower, althoug it has an observation deck o top and is a popular touris attraction. On a clear da visitors can see nearly 7 miles in any direction-including the mist from Nia gara Falls.

The Petronius Platform an oil-drilling rig in the Gu of Mexico, is 2,001 feet hig but only 225 of that is abov water.

The KVLY-TV transmi ting tower in Fargo, Nort Dakota, is a 2,063-foot-hig antenna. Since it is sup ported by anchor wires, th tower is not considered freestanding structure.

N PLANET EARTH

DAMS

The Rogun Dam in Tajikistan is the highest dam in the world at 1,100 feet. It sits across the Vaksh River and is constructed primarily of dirt and rock. Tajikistan is one of the smallest and poorest countries in Central Asia, and it is completely landlocked. Interestingly, the second-highest dam in the world, the Nurek Dam, is also in Tajikistan.

BRIDGES

The world's highest bridge is the Millau Viaduct in France. At its highest point, the bridge is 1,125 feet, just slightly shorter than the Empire State Building. The distance from the roadway to the River Tarn below is 886 feet. (That's almost the same height as the X-Scream, our vote for world's scariest ride.)

The causeway over Lake Ponchartrain in Louisiana is nearly 24 miles from start to finish, making it the world's longest bridge. It runs from Metairie, just outside of New Orleans, to Mandeville. The bridge is really an elevated roadway, sitting only several feet above the water on 9,000 concrete risers. Once you're on it, you have to go all the way to the end because there is no way to turn around.

The longest suspension bridge, supported by wires and towers, is Japan's Akashi-Kaikyo Bridge, which crosses 200 feet above the Akashi Strait. It is 6,532 feet long between its two support towers. The cables that hold up the bridge are made up of 37,000 strands of thin wire, and the total length of the cables is more than 186,000 miles—which would stretch three quarters of the way from the Earth to the moon.

PLANES

The Ukrainian An-225 Cossack is the largest airplane in the world, and was designed to carry the Soviet space shuttle in the 1990s. The Cossack has a wingspan of 291 feet (just 9 feet short of a football field), is 276 feet long, and weighs nearly 200 tons. Today, it is used for transporting incredibly heavy cargo like locomotive trains. Its wingspan is twice as long as the Wright Brothers' first airplane.

SHIPS

The longest passenger ship ever built is the *Queen Mary II*, launched in 2003. It is 1,132 feet long and, if stood on its end, would be just a hundred feet shorter than the Empire State Building.

The *Knock Nevis*, a supertanker for transporting oil, is the world's largest ship, with a length of 1,504 feet and a width of 226 feet. Tipped on end, it would be taller than every building in the world except for Taipei 101 and Burj Dubai. It weighs over 500,000 tons. In contrast, the average car weighs about two tons.

WALLS

The Great Wall of China is the largest structure ever created by man, running 3,948 miles from start to finish, longer than the width of the United States. The first part of the wall was begun around 500 B.C. and construction took place on and off for the next 1,000 years.

THINGS YOU DIDN'T KNO

☑ Holland is not a country. It is part of the Netherlands, although most people refer to the Netherlands as Holland. People from this country are called Dutch.

☑ The heart of a blue whale can weigh almost a ton, or as much as a big motorcycle.

☑ The Golden Gate Bridge is not gold, it is a dark, orange-red color. The name Golden Gate comes from the name of the water beneath it, the Golden Gate Strait—it was the water "gateway" into California from the Pacific Ocean, and resembled a similar strait in Istanbul called the Golden Horn.

☑ Spiders are not insects. They are arachnids and have two body segments and eight legs. Insects, like ants, have three body segments and six legs.

☑ Spit can freeze to ice in midair in certain parts of the Arctic.

☑ Your stomach uses hydrochloric acid to break down your food. Hydrochloric acid is used to corrode steel, which means that your stomach acid could eat through the outside of a car.

☑ The giant bullfrog of South Africa, which weighs more than four pounds, has been known to attack lions.

☑ Your body contains 60,000 miles of blood vessels, enough to wrap around the world almost three times.

☑ The average pencil can draw a line more than 30 miles long.

☑ The "black box" used on airplanes to record flight information in case of an accident is actually an orange cylinder.

☑ If you started spelling out all the numbers, the first time you would get to the letter A is at 1,000 (one thousand).

☑ A tiger's skin is striped exactly like its fur.

☑ There is more computing power in a modern laptop computer than NASA had in all of the computers it used to put men on the moon in 1969.

☑ Your body contains enough iron to make a two-inch-long nail.

☑ The 100 Years War between France and England lasted 116 years.

☑ An angry grizzly bear ca run as fast as a horse.

☑ Jell-O, which is a tast gelatin food, is made from animal skins and bones. S are some glues.

☑ Scientists know mor about the visible univers than they do about how ou brains work.

☑ The first living creatur sent into space was a do named Laika. She wa launched aboard *Sputnik* on November 3, 1957. Yu Gagarin, the first man i space, didn't go up until 196

☑ After frogs shed thei skin, they eat it.

☑ Glass is considered eithe a slow-moving liquid or fast-moving solid, whic helps explain why you ca see through glass. The mole cules in glass move fas enough that you can se through it (like a liquid), bu move slow enough that the can be formed into shape (like a solid).

☑ $111,111,111 \times 111,111,11 = 12,345,678,987,654,321$

☑ The opposite sides of dic always add up to seven.

ВUT PROBABLY SHOULD)

☑ When you're full-grown, our brain weighs as much s a jar of peanut butter.

☑ "Pneumonoultramicro-copicsilicovolcanoconiosis" is word that refers to a kind of ung disease. It is the longest vord in the English language. Pronounce it like this: new-noe-no-ultra-microscopic-sil-co-volcano-coney-oh-sis.

☑ Chess originated in Per-ia (present-day Iran), and the word "checkmate" comes from the phrase "*shah mat,*" which means "the king is dead."

☑ The Popsicle was invented in 1905 by Frank Epperson, an 11-year-old boy. He left a soda with a stirring stick in it on his porch overnight . . . and it froze.

☑ Americans eat 350 slices of pizza a second, or 17.4 million square feet per day—enough pizzas to cover a large farm or about 10 city blocks by 10 city blocks. All told, that equals three billion pizzas per year—10 pizzas for every single person in the country, including babies.

☑ Spiders have clear blood.

☑ The Taj Mahal, a domed building in India over 100 feet high, is not a palace. It is a mausoleum where the builder's wife is buried.

THE SIMPLE COIN VANISH

Hold a coin with the thumb and first finger of your LEFT hand.

Drag your RIGHT hand over the coin and your LEFT hand fingers. Do this so that the fingers of your RIGHT hand face your audience.

Quickly close your RIGHT hand and pull it away as if snatching the coin from your LEFT hand, but don't really grab the coin. By making the snatch-and-grab motion, and then leading the audience's eyes with your RIGHT hand, you are creating the illusion that you have grabbed the coin with your RIGHT hand.

Holding your RIGHT hand up in the air, slowly open it and reveal that the coin is gone!

What happened is that while you dragged your RIGHT hand over the coin, you were providing a shield so that the coin could drop unseen from your fingers into the palm of your LEFT hand.

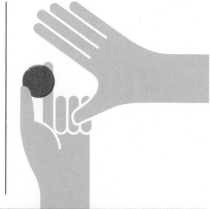

Some people pocket the coin in the LEFT hand while they are waving their RIGHT hand. Others quickly reach over to someone's ear with their LEFT hand and pretend to grab the coin from there. Either way, practice makes the trick perfect.

IP NEWQUIST has authored more than a dozen books for both children and adults, including the critically acclaimed *The Great Brain Book*. It was cited by the ational Science Teachers Association and the Children's Book Council as one of the outanding science books of 2006, and was named as one of the best books for young readers by ne American Library Association.

To prepare for writing *For Boys Only*, Mr. Newquist went scuba diving with sharks in Ausalia, climbed the Great Wall of China, drove some really fast cars, learned a few magic tricks, nd read more books than he can count.

or more, go to **www.newquistbooks.com**.

MARC ARONSON has the good fortune of writing and editing books on ubjects he loves researching—such as American History, archaeology, sports, and, well, cool stuff r boys. His biography *Sir Walter Ralegh and the Quest for El Dorado* (Clarion, 2000) won the Amer-an Library Association's first-ever Robert Sibert Medal for excellence in nonfiction, as well as ne Boston Globe—Horn Book Prize. Most recently, he went to Stonehenge to work on a book with team of archaeologists doing new research on the site. He frequently speaks at schools, has been atured on Book TV, and maintains a blog called "Nonfiction Matters" at SLJ.com. In 2006, he erved as the History Channel's local spokesman for its Save Our History program. He lives with s wife and two sons in New Jersey.

or more, go to **www.marcaronson.com**.